**RESURRECT Y
CELEBRAT**

SHE HAS RISEN

Tanya Sood

She Has Risen
Copyright © 2017 by Tanya Sood

No part of this publication may be reproduced, distributed, or transmitted in any form or by any means, including photocopying, recording, or other electronic or mechanical methods, without the prior written permission of the author, except in the case of brief quotations embodied in critical reviews and certain other non-commercial uses permitted by copyright law.

Tellwell Talent
www.tellwell.ca

ISBN
978-1-77370-220-9 (Hardcover)
978-1-77370-219-3 (Paperback)
978-1-77370-221-6 (eBook)

This is dedicated to my friend Amy Gusso and to my coach, Guy Reichard, who were like my midwife and midhusband, supporting and encouraging me to birth this book.

To my husband, Robert, who helped me conceive it.

To my daughter, Georgia, who I hope will resurrect her Divine Feminine wisdom, and truly own and celebrate it. And to my son, Everett, who I hope will respect and honour all those who have the courage to unleash it.

Table of Contents

Introduction 9
1. Acknowledge Your Divinity 17
2. Understand Your Values 37
3. Quiet Your Mind and Set Intentions 51
4. Heal Your Mother Wounds 67
5. Assemble a Sisterhood 85
6. Overcome Fear 101
7. Take Action and Receive Divine Gifts 113
8. Have Faith 127
9. Accept and Love Yourself, Girl! 143
10. Be Grateful and Filled with Awe and Wonder 159
11. Celebrate and Feel Good 173
12. Give Back 189

Acknowledgements 197
About the Author 201
Bibliography 203
Notes 207

"Woman is the radiance of God; she is not your beloved. She is the Creator—you could say that she is not created."

~ RUMI

Introduction

I didn't even know what the Divine Feminine was on my twenty-sixth birthday when I stepped up, in heels, onto a wobbly patio table at a crowded bar, held my drink in the air and shouted, "Cheers! To my vagina!" But looking back, I'm quite certain she surged through me that night. As she often does—like a lightning rod! What I do know is that I haven't been the same since.

At the time, I wasn't sure if it was the red wine or the moonlight, the summer breeze or how easily those bold words catapulted from loins to lungs, but I felt so confident! So alive! So proud and powerful, as if I unlocked something deep within me that had been waiting for years to surge out. Of course, I didn't know it then—I just thought it was something wild and funny I said (you should've seen the look on my friends' faces!). Only in hindsight did I realize that she came to me at a time when I was ready to step into my power. And really own it.

Looking back, sixteen years later, I realize that in many ways I opened Pandora's Box that night. Well, maybe not

Pandora's but my own. I recall a Greek mythology class where I learned about Zeus, god of gods, who ordered Prometheus to create the first woman on Earth. They named her Pandora meaning 'all-gifted' because of her long list of virtues. *This is what the story was about in the beginning, my friends: a girl who was stacked.* But an eighth-century poem by Hesiod gave Pandora prominence when he called her out in the interest of shifting the power from earlier goddesses who were sovereign. That's right – he was trying to change *her*story into *his*tory. The poem was an attempt to swing the pendulum back to establish a patriarchal order among the gods, with Zeus at the reigns. It was a deliberate effort to poach power and exploit goddesses and earthly women at the pleasure of the male gods.

It's fair to say that the role of women in Hesiod's poem was exceptionally subordinate. I mean who's kidding who: the guy was a full-out misogynist. And Erasmus of Rotterdam—a Catholic priest, social critic, teacher, and theologian — translated Pandora's story from Hesiod's work to only perpetuate disdain toward women. Erasmus also denied women power when he boxed in Pandora through his translation of the Greek word for *pithos* meaning 'honey vase' – let's take a wild guess at what *that* might have meant – into the Latin word of *pyxis* meaning 'box.' And box is what stuck. Or should I say, where we as women got stuck. Not to mention boxed in.

Now, for centuries scholars have been on a wild goose chase trying to decode the meaning of this and other similar stories. Many have concluded that curiosity killed the cat. Respect authority. We must do as we're told and avoid temptation. Others (read: misogynists) argue that the story of Pandora's box is further evidence that the origin of evil in the universe traces back to the creation of *women*. They liken it to the book of Genesis where Eve too was warned not to eat the forbidden fruit but surrendered to her natural-born tendencies.

What strikes me most about the stories of Pandora, Eve and Mary Magdalene is that they were written by *men*! And I don't mean the men of today's era—many of whom have evolved and garner respect for both genders, valuing the unique qualities each possesses to make this world whole—men like my husband. No. I'm talking about the men of an era when dominant forces and those in positions of authority vigilantly suppressed women and tried to contain their truth and power. After all, life is created *through* women. Really, what greater power than life force exists?

What bothers me deeply is that in schools today, little girls (like my daughter) are learning about this mythological figure, Pandora, who was a bad girl because she opened a box she wasn't supposed to and then poof! all the evil of the world flew out—it's all our fault. Thank goodness for the little hope that was left at the bottom to save the rest of humanity. Phew!

What today's little girls aren't being taught is that the *myth* of Pandora's box was written by a Greek poet who was desperately trying to help men re-claim power, which he believed women owned at the time (poor guy didn't realize that power is abundant and doesn't require one group to steal from another for both to possess it). The story was translated to the point of being re-written in the fifteenth century by a dude who was trying, along with the Catholic Church, to snuff out women's power all while struggling to live his own truth (he was in the closet) in the confines of the Catholic Church, which regarded homosexuality as sin that needed to be rejected. Oh, and they have a problem with women too.

Thomas Aquinas didn't help matters. He said women were intellectually inferior, with scripture — also written, translated and copied by male priests – as his guide. He drew on examples such as 1 Corinthians 11:10 where it states that "man was not created for the sake of woman, but woman was created for the sake of man.[1]" I wonder what it would have said if wise nuns held the reed and ink. Augustine's view of women in the thirteenth century, along with Aristotle assumptions of gender, further diminished women's position. For Aristotle and Aquinas, women were intrinsically inferior, biologically considered as incomplete human beings. Women couldn't represent normative humanity – only men – and so Christ had to be a male. These dudes were of the opinion that women couldn't be ordained because they couldn't represent Christ, and they certainly couldn't be leaders. After all, they lacked autonomous humanness and they had to be always under male authority, don't you know.

Forgive me, girls, as I pause for a moment to take a breath. Because this shit makes me hot. Red hot angry hot. Because it's so...far... from the *TRUTH*! It's a big, hissing, foul-smelling lie! *This* is the shit that came out of Pandora's box. *This* is the shit that needed to come out to be exposed. *This* is the evil that women have to "let out" by opening the box of their own *power*. *This* is the shit that makes us want to slam the lid shut because it can seem too scary for some, too boat-rocking, too difficult to face. Too David and Goliath. But we know how *that* story ended. The truth is: there never was a box.

Just like Pandora, we were made perfect and blessed with an abundance of virtues. It was *people* who created the boxes – men, women and even ourselves. But despite this, there is still hope. We know that at the bottom of those boxes, there will always be hope.

Thank heavens, my friends, that times they are a-changing. As the Chinese proverb suggests, "When sleeping women wake, mountains move." That's what happened on the night of my twenty-sixth birthday. It was the beginning of my internal awakening when I quite literally stepped up and into my own power and wisdom. I didn't do this alone. There was something that had been like a sleeping dragon inside me that was just finally ready to wake up. And when it happens to you – and maybe it already has – watch out, because things will never be the same. It's a transformation for the better but in my experience, it doesn't happen overnight or without a fight.

This book has been nineteen years in the making. The idea of writing a book hit my heart (hard) when I was twenty-three; the Divine Feminine started to awake within me at twenty-six; and for the past sixteen years, I have been struggling and fighting off all of the demons and discoveries that have landed me in many different therapists' chairs, in the corporate world, in (and out of) seminary and a world of places in between. Honestly, I have felt pregnant with this book for nineteen years. You should see my cankles. And now I'm at the point where it's hurting me – I'm in labour with it – my water has broken and I'm writing my way through the canal and into the place of hope.

What I know now – and what I didn't know then – is the truth about Pandora's Box. The truth is, it's a *myth*. Greek mythology – just like it says. And recognizing that was the first step in starting a remarkable journey of unlocking my own power and the essence of the Divine Feminine wisdom that slept for so long inside me but has now awakened and is just waiting to come out. You holding this book in your hands and reading these words is evidence that you are exactly where you are meant to be at exactly the right time, and she is awakening within you too. We can ride this leg of the journey together. And as for all that ugly stuff that's exposed – it's the devil we know and nothing new that we can't wade through together.

That night of my twenty-sixth birthday, *"Cheers to my vagina!"* practically came to life for me, and with that realization, I knew it was much more than a phrase. I've come to realize it's more than me. It's a rally cry. We as women are the chalices – the receptacle – and we need to be filled with her Divine nectar. We are sensual warrioresses and this is our story. It's about acknowledging and empowering our inner goddesses to charge through us like wild, beautiful lightening, re-energizing our force fields, restoring our power and redefining the limits of what we thought was possible.

This book is also all about boxes: Pandora's box, Pauline theology (which mostly excludes women), our own boxes, and rising out of them. It's about quite literally our own boxes – a.k.a. our vaginas – and opening the power that is found right between our legs! By virtue of being a woman, by virtue of unleashing what has always been ours, what is coming to life now, what is awakening and finding voice and cause and presence within our world, we can open the waterfall of virtues that spring from its well. This is our birthright. This is what we were put on this earth to be.

It is my sincere hope that *She Has Risen* will stir a positive, powerful revolution within the bodies, minds and spirits of more women than I can count so that together, we can stand in strength, dignity, honour and sass-tacularness and raise our glasses to our wild, wise and Divine selves and for the love of humanity—*Cheers, to our vaginas!* But mostly, it's my deepest hope that this book will set the record straight regarding stories like those of Pandora, Eve and Mary Magdalene who were scapegoats to absolve chauvinists of any responsibility or blame for the evils of the world.

I'm not a man-hater, and I know that all men aren't like this. But throughout history, enough men in power acted upon false information, which led us to this corrupted state. It's time to set the truth free so our daughters, coming up the path and into their own, will be able to spot the myths, realize the truth and educate their teachers, classmates and friends about what this shit is and what it isn't so they can stay true to their paths and not let roadblocks, distractions, anything or anyone stop them from becoming all they are meant to be for themselves and for this world. As the mother of a six-year-old daughter, this means to world to me. And so my wish for my daughter, Georgia, whose name means 'tiller of soil or farmer' is that she will resurrect her own Divine Feminine wisdom and discover the wellspring of hope that lives inside and feeds the abundance of good seeds within her.

Each chapter of this book describes the journey I've been on to fully accept and unleash my Divine Feminine wisdom and power (which continues to be a work-in-progress). My hope is that these words will inspire you to do the same. Because we need you. The world needs all of you. Unabashed, wild and free.

1
Acknowledge Your Divinity

> "Femininity is part of the God-given divinity within each of you. It is your incomparable power and influence to do good. You can, through your supernal gifts, bless the lives of children, women, and men. Be proud of your womanhood. Enhance it. Use it to serve others."
>
> ~ JAMES E. FAUST

Let me start by confessing magister quod discipulus, or in plain English, 'teacher is student' here, my friends. I fight the urge to scoff at myself for even writing a chapter titled "Acknowledge Your Divinity" because I am ever so slowly learning this lesson myself. Spiritually, I accept the argument that a divine spark of energy exists and is living within me—within each of us. Intellectually, it makes sense that the more attention I give it, the more it will grow. When I take these thoughts and layer in the mystery of hope, I can even appreciate its potential to blaze with stunning glory and spill out into the world to serve others. Scripture says, "Do you not know that you are a temple of God and that the Spirit of God dwells in you?" (1 Corinthians 3:16)² and I believe it.

Divinity isn't earned; it's deeply entrenched in the essence of our beings. But sometime—oh sometimes—those thoughts aren't enough to comfort me in the still dark night when I'm restless and doubt, fear and worry set in.

What's getting me through is this newfound belief that my divinity doesn't actually live in my thoughts—it lives in my body. The temple. Even that realization has been tough to swallow because in many ways, I have been rejecting my body for more years than I care to admit. Again, intellectually I can concede that *hello!* This body has been good to me for forty-two years. I am healthy! I am alive! I am strong and mobile and all my parts work! I have conceived, carried, birthed and fed two healthy babies. I can do cartwheels and twist my tongue into a three-leaf clover. I have orgasms!

This body is good and I am grateful. But then, there are times when I walk by a mirror or catch my reflection in the window, and all of these judgments rush in. About that fountain of grey roots springing from the part of my hair or the acne that has nestled on my left cheek or the wrinkles that stretch across my forehead, the skin tags on my neck, the sinking breasts, the rounded abdomen that I think sometimes makes me still look pregnant. All these horrible thoughts! Again, in my head, I know they aren't helpful. Not kind. Not loving or accepting or even necessarily true. Why am I doing this to myself? And what if my children – particularly my daughter – heard my judgments about myself in this way? Knowing she looks up to me (for now anyway), what if she internalizes *my* internal dialogue and turns on herself? Oh! It would just eat me up inside if that ever happened. So I know in my head that I need to move past this stumbling block, for me and especially for her – but how do I do it?

It's through my body. It has always been through the body. My body is a temple – the container of my soul. How do I know this for sure? Well, I had to go and do a little research (back into my head again, I know—I can take a lot of convincing). But what I learned shocked me—stopped me right in my tracks. It confused and bewildered me, and I'm still reeling in awe and wonder about it. And then, before I could even look back, it turned me into a believer. Here's what happened.

Sacred geometry

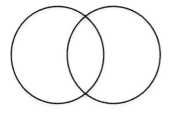

Vesica piscis

I discovered sacred geometry and its link to the body. I discovered the *vesica piscis* and it is *blowing my mind*. I didn't even know it was 'thing!' If you're new to this too, the vesica piscis is that shape found at the intersection of two disks with the same radius. They intersect in such a way that the centre of each disk lies on the perimeter of the other. In Latin, the term vesica piscis translates to the 'bladder of a fish.' In Italian, it's called a *mandorla*, that almond shape that symbolizes the pairing of two worlds: y'know...the sacred and the earthly! Um, hello nebula. Eye of the Universe much? Pin drop.

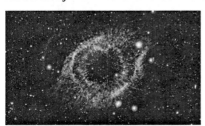

Eye of the Universe

So, what does that have to do with the body? Every single thing that exists in this universe springs out of the shape of the vesica piscis, the womb of all creation. Like God and Goddess joined together to create an offspring. And it turns out that the vesica piscis shape is found all *over* the body. For example, the shape of our eyes—and everything you see that comes through them—vesica piscis. It's the shape of our mouths—and p.s. all the energy our bodies need comes through our mouths. It's found in the shape of our ears—and everything we hear comes through the ears, in particular, music.

Music enthusiasts may be delighted to know that the mandorla corresponds with the dominant interval (G, B in C-major), which is often used in musical composition to create tension and resolve or harmony. It chains together a series of chords that form the Cycle of Fifths. When represented as a lattice of interlocking vesica piscis, these dominant triads can be seen to cascade through an orbit of twelve tones—and traces out to resemble the profile of a fish!

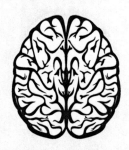

Two Hemispheres of the Brain

The two hemispheres of the brain take the shape of the vesica piscis. Interestingly, the right side is known for its intuition, creativity, compassion, emotion, creativity, empathy, collaboration, spirituality and holistic thought—all feminine energy. Whereas the left side is known for analytical and rational thinking, competition, determination, linear thinking, logical thought, and action—all masculine energy. The hypothalamus and, of particular note, the pineal gland correspond to this shape as well. The pineal gland is a small endocrine gland in the vertebrate brain that produces serotonin and melatonin, hormones that affect mood and modulate our wake/sleep patterns and seasonal functions. Its shape resembles a tiny pinecone (hence its Latin name *pinea*, which means 'pinecone'), and it's located near the centre of the brain between the two hemispheres, tucked in a groove where the two rounded thalamic bodies join (the vesica piscis!)

In fact, when you trace the shapes of the glands associated with each sacred chakra—the testes in men and ovaries in women, the adrenal glands, the pancreas, thymus, thyroid, pituitary and pineal glands—they are *all* shaped like the vesica piscis. Hot damn! There is sacred divinity found all over our body. We are Divine beings. It's etched all over our bodies. I know life gets busy and we can easily get into a rut with things. Maybe that's the last thing you want to think about on those days when your kid has just been sick and you're vacuuming up puke while trying to call your boss, but maybe it's in those moments we need a reminder the most that we are Divine beings. We are Divine! Puke stains and all!

The Eye of Horus

It's no wonder the Egyptians have been trying to catch our attention for centuries with this shape and its significance. The *Ankh*! It's known as the breath of life, the key of the Nile and the ancient hieroglyphic character that read 'life.' It appears in either the hand of or in proximity to almost every deity in the Egyptian pantheon, including the pharaohs. And then there's the Eye of Horus! Its shape is totally linked to the pineal gland and is associated with dreaming, psychic ability and the third eye. When we meditate, we're engaging our pineal gland. It's related to third-eye experiences. Plato, Descartes, Buddha were all onto it. In fact, look atop a Buddha head and you'll see that same shape – it looks like tiny pinecones and symbolizes the pineal gland and the awakening of the third eye. It's punctuated by the dot that's found in the middle of Buddha's forehead, something us East Indians have worn for centuries in the form of a bindi to acknowledge the third eye, which represents the universe, the sixth chakra, *ajna*, and the seat of "concealed wisdom." Is any of this blowing your mind too?

The Bible even references it in Jesus's quotes in Matthew 6:22: "The light of the body is the eye; therefore if thine eye be single, thy whole body shall be full of light."[3] Not to mention again in Matthew 4:16 when he states: "The people which sat in darkness saw great light."[4]

And advanced civilizations that existed thousands of years before Christ was even on the scene – such as the Egyptians, Sumerians, Annunaki and Babylonians – used the sacred pinecone symbol throughout their artwork. The back of the American dollar bill even depicts reference to the third eye – *why haven't I noticed this before?*

You'll find the symbol of the pinecone all over the place in the Vatican. The Pope even carries a depiction of it on his staff. Look at Renaissance art! Leonardo DaVinci's art: the *Vitruvian Man*, even the *Mona Lisa* and *The Last Supper* have patterns that call out the third eye when they are overlaid with sacred geometry.

Next time you're in a church, look up at the stained glass images and paintings symbolizing moments that transcend time and space – Resurrection, Transfiguration and the Dormition of the Theotokos – and there you'll see figures such as Jesus, Mary and others encased in a mandorla. Why? What is the other part of the body that can be found within the vesica piscis and is shaped like a mandorla? The shape of a woman's womb. The shape of a vagina—or as some would call it—that inter-dimensional door we all cross through in spirit form. And that's when my holy shit moment happened.

The adoration of cavemen, artists and architects—oh my!

Back to the vagina where my whole spiritual awakening was born. While the vagina's mystique has been exploited, jaded and distorted over time, it only takes a walk through history—and prehistory—to understand how others knew, respected and adored her. We've uncovered that cave men carved vaginal images into rocks dating back to 35,000 B.C. Neanderthals even knew she was one to watch. And through the centuries that moved us from prehistoric to historic times, art has been sculpted, painted and drawn in her honour. Leonardo da Vinci added to the Renaissance's cultural and scientific reawakening with his 1510 rendering of *The Female Sexual*. And that's not all. From Goya's 1797-1800 *La Maja Desnuda* and Gustave Courbet's 1866 provocative *L'Origine du Monde* to Egon Schiele's 1910 *Reclining Female Nude with Violet Stockings* and his 1911 *Girl with Black Hair* – each recognized the beauty, power and precociousness of the vagina. Gustav Klimt, Alfred Stieglitz, Georgia O'Keeffe, Christiane Schad and Marcel Duchamp all added to this collection, immortalizing the Divine vagina (vag-divina?) through art.

Architects love her form and function too. I mean, think about it. Qatar's World Cup Stadium? Looks like a vagina. Chicago's Crain Communications Building? Skyscraping vagina! Rem Koolhaas's CCTV building in China? Vag-er-ific. San Francisco MoMA? Vag-lightful. And honest to God, the Cathedral of Christ the Light in Oakland, California? It's practically a vigil to the vagina. Norman Foster's Spaceport in New

Mexico—ole! It's a vagina! I could go on. The Eiffel Tower even looks like a vagina to me. Throw a mandorla around it and it's got that, how'd you say, uh...*je ne sais quoi*. But I digress.

Cathedral of Christ the Light in Oakland

Just look around through this altered lens and you'll see what I mean. She's architecturally, structurally and artfully sound. She radiates life, and for that and many other reasons, she deserves the world's respect, honour and appreciation for all she is and all she has always been. Gustave Courbet said it best (and how lovely it would be to hear it roll off the tongue in French): "L'Origine du Monde." That's what she is, 'the origin of the world,' people. The gateway to humanity! The vag-force. The motherload. Ancient civilizations have known this. Mathematicians, scientists, physicists and spiritual leaders all know this. The Vatican knows this. Now it's time for us to know and own this. Divinity and life force lives within you and me. And it's tucked right inside our honey pots. Its power and life force have always been there, since the beginning of time. And some of us have quite literally been sitting on this power without even knowing it.

Sacred vessel for the soul

In Sumerian hymns that praised women as goddess, the vagina was often called a "boat of heaven," a vessel meant to carry the most wonderful gifts from heaven to earth. *In Praise of the Goddess: The Devimahatmaya and Its Meaning*, is where Devadatta Kali writes about the ancient Indian text, the

Devimahatmaya, from sixteen centuries ago, which identified the womb as floating mid-ocean, extending through the sky and bringing creative power to earth. The Divine Mother and her boat of a vagina are considered the centre of the universe. And so when it comes to my body, and especially my vagina—where this whole spiritual awakening started—I'm now a believer that there is divinity within me.

As Psalm 139: 13-14 suggests, "For you formed my inward parts; you knitted me together in my mother's womb. I praise you, for I am fearfully and wonderfully made."[5] This passage emphasizes the incredible nature of our physical bodies. Many would argue that the human body is the most complex and unique organisms in the world, and that its complexity and uniqueness speaks volumes about the mind of its Divine Creator. Everything has its place, everything has a function and every aspect of the body, down to the tiniest microscopic cell, reveals that it is fearfully and wonderfully made. Each cell, once called a "simple" cell, is a tiny factory not yet fully understood by humans. Why is this? I believe it's about that awe-factor! It's about keeping us in a state of awe and wonder, which is important. So important I dedicated a chapter to it. I need to remember that state of awe I felt when I was pregnant with a belly filled with the creation of human life itself. Our bodies are truly amazing. *My* body is truly amazing—yours is too. I've come to appreciate that and now must honour it.

Feminine meets masculine

Another example: the two standard sex symbols denoting male and female are derived from astrological symbols denoting the classical planet of Mars and Venus. What's found between them when they're linked together? You got it – it's the vesica piscis. The intersection of these two overlapping spheres (including the interior and two-dimensional version) represent, among other things: the vagina, the joining of God and Goddess to create an offspring, the symbol for Jesus Christ (and Mary Magdalene, but that's another book), the basic motif in the flower of life, an overlay in the Tree of Life and a source of immense power and energy.

Part of acknowledging divinity involves not only honouring the physical body but the Divine presence – both masculine and feminine – that exists within our bodies.

It's important to note that the Divine Feminine energy doesn't necessarily represent the female human body and the Divine Masculine energy doesn't necessarily represent the male human body. Each of us has both the Divine Feminine and Divine Masculine energy inside us. If this weren't the case, we would not have logical thought and creativity. One of the first ways to balance your Divine Feminine and Divine Masculine energy is to understand the differences between them. This awareness will lead to an awareness of your thoughts, so you don't subconsciously think too much with your left or right brain. Another important discovery involves determining what Divine Feminine and Divine Masculine qualities you lack and then taking actions toward strengthening them in a way that creates balance between the two sacred energies. Meditating is a great way to balance these energies.

Unfortunately, for centuries the feminine part of the equation hasn't been given the attention it needs and deserves in this male-centric world and within most religious sects. So what exactly is this Divine Feminine thing all about? In recent years, she's certainly turned heads, weaving her way through threads of conversations within our culture, spirituality and lives. But she is older than the hills! Pure wisdom herself. In fact, glimpses of her can be found nestled in Proverbs 8:1-4, 22-31 in the Old Testament:

> Does not wisdom call, and does not understanding raise her voice? On the heights, beside the way, at the crossroads she takes her stand; beside the gates in front of the town, at the entrance of the portals she cries out: "To you, O people, I call, and my cry is to all that live.
>
> The Lord created me at the beginning of his work, the first of his acts of long ago. Ages ago I was set up, at the first, before the beginning of earth. When there were no depths I was brought forth, when there were no springs abounding with water. Before the mountains had been shaped, before the hills, I was brought forth – when he had not yet made earth and fields, or the world's first bits of soil. When he established the heavens, I was there, when he drew a circle on the face of the deep, when he made firm the skies above, when he established the fountains of the deep, when he assigned to the sea its limit, so that the waters might not transgress his command, when he marked out the foundations of the earth, then I was beside him, like a master worker; and I was daily his

delight, rejoicing before him always, rejoicing in his inhabited world and delighting in the human race."[6]

This passage is particularly inspiring today as many consider this a time of reawakening and returning to higher frequencies of light and thought, like those found within this passage on wisdom. Some have questioned if it's Christian, Buddhist, Pagan or New Age. Is it tied to religion or is it a spiritual concept? But the Divine Feminine isn't a *concept* and she can't be put into a box—forgive the pun. (Everyone knows she comes *out* of a box anyway!) She's the feminine side of the one God—Source, Universe, whatever your description—that has existed in all traditions since the beginning of time. And after thousands of years of dormancy, people are starting to recognize traces of her within themselves. And that is why so many of us are starting to wake up to her now.

Why now?

In ancient times, women were revered as strong, beautiful, creative and sensual beings. Being keenly attuned to the primal rhythm of the planet was necessary for mere human survival. We relied on our ability to live in harmony with our surroundings. The Sacred Feminine was honoured then, and women were considered a symbol of life itself.

But the world changed. Gifts inherent to women were lost or set aside while gifts of the masculine were revered and made central. The balance shifted.

Today we're in the midst of another great shift. My astrologer friend tells me that 2012 marked the beginning of a 26,000-year cycle known as the Aquarian Age. During this cycle, the sun is moving its way back through the signs of the zodiac. It's a gradual shift in the earth's rotation on its axis. Old ways are ending. We've moved past humanity's tipping point and we're in a new age of the Divine Feminine. It's time to tap into that ancient feminine energy that was honoured for its intuition, wisdom, creation, collaboration, sensuality and even blessing. By welcoming this role as sisters and co-creators of the future, women bless themselves and each another, encouraging more women to welcome feminine energy in themselves.

Drop the "He"

Over the past few years, as I've moved into embracing and honouring my own Divine Feminine energy, some major core beliefs have shifted and changed my way of thinking and behaving. I can't even describe God as "He" anymore—it's inaccurate in my view. Thankfully, many churches are now honouring this as well and changing the He references to God references. The priests came up with He! God is not male or female, mother or father. God is God and God is both. Like the yin and yang energies, the Divine Feminine side of God complements life's balance. She's a powerful part of primal Mother Earth, symbolizing balance, healing, renewal and restoration. And she exists within each of us—women *and* men. This divinity needs to be acknowledged to find balance in our lives.

Androgynous India

Growing up with an East Indian father, I was always fascinated when we'd visit relatives' homes. As a child, I'd go exploring throughout the house to discover the many different shrines nestled in corners of rooms. I'd often find alters adorned with candles and incense, prayer pillows and pictures of deities that looked both male and female to me. So many of India's sculptures, paintings and spiritual figures are neither masculine nor feminine —they're both. I found all of this so remarkable, comforting and confusing at the same time.

As a young adult, learning more about these deities piqued my curiosity, so I took a few university courses on eastern religions. I could write piles of essays on these topics, but it wasn't until I ventured to India that I really began to understand the broad spectrum of spirituality, religion, the power of the Divine Feminine and her grace.

India simply took my breath away. It is a most awe-inspiring country, sheer intensity for each of the senses— and senses I didn't even know I had. A part of me felt so ignited and alive there, something I hadn't ever experienced in Western society. In many ways, going to India was like waking up for me, particularly when it came to expressing and understanding more about my Divine Feminine power and wisdom. It's like Mother Nature brought me home to India, and this incredible country helped me acknowledge the divinity that exists within me and within each of us.

I spent time in an ashram in Rishikesh, nestled deep in the Himalayan mountains, where each morning and evening, my husband and I would gather with two hundred orphans and other pilgrims for *aarrti,* the daily ritual prayers. They took place along the Gungaji, the Ganges River. And as we offered ourselves, our thoughts, desires, actions and things to God, I'd find myself staring at the androgynous statue of Krishna that was so revered that it rose several storeys above the water. We'd sing songs, clap our hands and praise this universal life force that captures all things as one. It was pure joy.

In Hindu India, the Divine Feminine power is not only recognized, it's honoured. Great rivers are named for goddesses. The ocean and the earth are considered the Mother, the trees her arms, the mountains her breasts, the plants her nourishment and the sky her lover.[7] In the Hindu tradition,

Mother as God is reflected in the names of Aditi, Devi, Gayatri, Kali, Kamala, Lakshmi, Parvati, Saraswati, Shakti and Usas. There are goddesses of the sun, dawn and starlit nights; there are goddesses of wealth and beauty, wisdom and aging, learning and speech, destruction and time. These goddesses are all considered an accepted and most treasured holy Mother. One of the most beautiful parts of Hinduism, I find, is that it embraces all spiritual traditions and sees all ways as valid paths to the supreme. It starts by recognizing that the entire creation springs from the Mother and that divinity lives within us.

Things changed considerably when the British came to rule India. They wanted to classify the many forms of worship that were practiced within the country, so they named the Muslims, Parsees, Sikhs and Jains. To the other religions, too numerous to designate, they gave the catchall name of Hindus. Of course, in those days, Indians saw all of the many ways of life, equal in value, as paths to enlightenment. There was a time when all these different religious groups worshipped side by side and in harmony with one another. And even today, the true Hindu embraces all religions and all spiritual practices as one.

On the Ganges I learned that when it comes to their faith, Hindus are very specific about one thing: Hinduism is not a dogma. It is a way of life. It permeates all aspects of their daily existence. From sunrise to sunset, in work, prayer and family life, Hinduism pervades everything they say, do and express.

A sobering return home to orthodox Christianity

After returning home from India and throughout the better part of my thirties, I started to deepen my understanding of my own spirituality and what truths resonated with me.

My husband was brought up Evangelical Lutheran and so I started attending church with him—I even went to Seminary to feed my curiosity. But I found myself stumbling on all this male dominance and female oppression, which just didn't fit with what I had learned in India. Why was Mary Magdalene's commanding influence during the formation of early Christianity all but erased from scriptures? Why was she commonly remembered as an unfortunate prostitute who simply underwent a conversion? Why wasn't she recognized as the great feminine force that even Jesus himself alludes to? And Mother Mary—why was she always portrayed with dowdy, demure, downcast eyes, dressed in pale blue and defined in terms of virgin purity? She used to wear red, just like Jesus. Why was she positioned as the mother of God and not worthy of being considered Mother as God? More importantly, why, by AD 200, was virtually all the feminine imagery for God removed from orthodox Christian tradition?

Conversely, in Hindu India, the Mother, who has been hidden in the shadow of Western religions for thousands of years, is considered the sum total of the energy in the universe. While today's India is mostly patriarchal, it wasn't always this way. More than three thousand years ago, during the Vedic age, women held positions of esteem in society. They shared equality with men and enjoyed liberal sanctions. The ancient Hindu philosophical concept of *shakti*, the feminine principle of energy, was born of this age. It took the form of worship of female idols or goddesses.

But the condition and status of women in India declined with the passage of time. During the medieval period, women were given a position subordinate to men. Law and religion didn't recognize the equal rights of men and women. And even when laws changed, rhetoric on paper was different than what was practiced. Women were shoehorned into the home and expected to be subservient to their husbands, the masters and rulers of the family. Having different inheritance laws for men and women became accepted practice as did the idea of a "marriageable age" (twenty-one for boys and eighteen for girls), no right to marital property, etc. And that's when everything went tits up so to speak.

It serves as an important warning for where we are in the world today. It can be a slippery slope when we allow the odd inappropriate comment, action or word slide. Normalizing can happen overnight. Jawaharlal Nehru, the leader of India's first Independence Movement and India's first prime minister, said it best when he declared, "You can tell the condition of a nation by looking at its women." It's true, and we all have a part to play here for the basic dignity and respect of our daughters and sisters coming up the path.

Throughout contemporary, historic and pre-historic times, many wise Hindus haven't stopped worshipping Mother—as well as Father. Having a living example of Mother worship in a major world religion can help us understand the power of the feminine force lost from Western spiritual traditions. It illuminates the path of the Mother. Her multifaceted appearances—from fierce to benevolent, seductive to repulsive—is all feminine expression. Some will welcome her polarity immediately, while others will need time to adjust to this wide range of emotions. But to accept this as a natural state, I invite you to consider changing weather patterns. I mean, if the weather can be rainy one minute and sunny or windy the next, why can't we?

Sanatana Dharma, the real name of Hinduism, means, 'the way of eternal truth.' It holds the belief that truth existed before humans, and the purpose of human beings, on whichever path, is to seek enlightenment. The unadulterated absolute which Hinduism brings to life, says everything and everyone comes from, lives in and goes to the same source—the river of love, the supreme soul, the eternal truth, the Great Mother.

East meets west

While my spirituality is still coming together today—and forever will be, for that matter—I'm not interested in a black or white, male or female, religion or practice. I'm interested in both and maybe all of these things. I'm interested in the truth, and I have a hunch that many others feel the same way. I'd even venture to say that Western society is starving for more of the Divine Feminine's influence. She teaches us to blow the limits and constraints off that dogma and liturgy that are often far too rigid and unforgiving.

The Divine Feminine is rising up in Western social discourse now more than ever. She has been oppressed for so long and finally, we're awakening to her as a society. She is rising within those who are open to her wisdom and power.

Acknowledging our divinity is about celebrating, honouring and owning this power so it can freely serve us, along with others we meet on our journeys. Because we *deserve* to own it. And we already do—it's our birthright. It's the power we've been blessed with as girls and women, and it's one that has been oppressed and contained within our society for so long now. But that's all changing. It's about basking in the glory of this power at our centre and allowing her to liberally course through our veins and boom! Right out of our cooches! It's about recognizing the beautiful life force—the balance of life—that exists within each of us. God—in both masculine and feminine forms—dwells within me, as me, and within you, as you.

CHAPTER 1 Reflections:

1. Have you had a moment when you sensed there was more than flesh, bones and tissue to your body but divinity within you as well? If so, describe it. If not, what has gotten in the way of you acknowledging your divinity?
2. How has the knowledge of the vesica piscis changed your view of your body?
3. What blows your mind about women's ability to mother or create life?
4. Are you noticing a stronger presence of Divine Feminine energy in the world today? If so, how? If not, what do you think is getting in the way?
5. How do you feel about the depiction—or absence—of women in scripture?
6. How could you more deeply honour your divinity?

2
Understand Your Values

"Your beliefs become your thoughts. Your thoughts become your words. Your words become your actions. Your actions become your habits. Your habits become your values. Your values become your destiny."

~ MAHATMA GANDHI

Attuning to your Divine Feminine wisdom means acknowledging your divinity, fully knowing yourself and your values and staying true to them. After all, it's our values—or what we believe—that are vital to the way we live, work and exist in this world. They determine our priorities, areas of focus and serve as a guide. They tell us where it would be wise to spend our time and energy. Our values can act like a measuring stick, helping us determine if our life is turning out the way we want it to, or *not*. Maybe the journey isn't so much about becoming anything, as that unknown saying goes. Maybe it's about un-becoming everything that isn't really you, so you can be who you were meant to be in the first place.

When we're living authentically, our values are expressed through almost every decision we make. They show up in the places we choose to work, where we invest our time, money and energy. They show up in our recreation and leisure activities, our social groups, spiritual connections, where we live and learn and how we operate in this world. They're part of the collection of *must-haves* in our lives. An underlying question for the process of uncovering your values is, "*What are the values you absolutely must honour or part of you dies?*"

They can be found in even the smallest details of our lives, for example, the candles we place on the dining room table. Are they real or are they artificial? If they are real, are they made of paraben, soy or beeswax? What colour are they? Where were they made? Where did you buy them? Or did you make them? Did you accept them as a gift? If so, from whom? The answers can serve as clues in detecting and reflecting our values. I used the candlestick analogy for a reason, as I have a real-life story to share about it.

Several years ago, when I was writing restaurant reviews for a local newspaper, I interviewed Bob Desautels, a successful business owner of four locavore-themed restaurants and pubs across Ontario. Bob experienced the candlestick dilemma himself. He knew he wanted candles on the tables of his restaurants for the ambiance, but he had a terrible time deciding which type to use. Staff members were trying to convince him to use flameless candles for insurance purposes and to avoid replacing them often. And while they were LED lights, which would complement his energy-reducing efforts—he runs on Bullfrog Power, Canada's 100% green energy provider—he felt conflicted about the plastic. They dramatically contrasted the wooden, Mennonite-crafted tables and chairs made from the reclaimed wood of a tree that came down on his property. It just seemed like an inauthentic pairing to him.

As we talked more about his values and interest in living in alignment with them, I suggested to Bob that maybe living this way leads to his ultimate happiness. "I'm not interested in living a happy life," Bob said, to my surprise. I asked him to tell me more. "Happiness is transient," he said. "I'm more interested in living a content life." Bob explained his response with an example. He said he had lost someone important to him, and he was very sad about it. But he still had this underlying feeling of contentment in his life. Bob is a person committed to expressing his values and beliefs through every decision he makes and living in alignment with his values served as a gateway to contentment.

Bob cares deeply about giving back to future generations, starting with his children and grandchildren. One of his favourite quotes is from Chief Seattle who said, "We don't inherit the earth; we borrow it from our children." Bob said that he started to believe that in a very visceral way when he had children and promised himself that when he did open a business, he'd express those values. Today all his restaurants are B Corps certified, which means they redefine success in business by meeting rigorous standards of social and environmental performance, accountability and transparency.

Bob's success accelerated after he took the time to contemplate and unearth his values. He explored. He took classes in everything from commerce to hotel management to craft brewing to the philosophy of religion, philosophy of the mind and introspection. After deeply contemplating, examining and recognizing his values, Bob gained clarity on who he was and what he needed to be and have in his life to thrive in this world. Today, The Neighbourhood Group, which he founded, is the umbrella organization that encompasses his restaurants, pubs, charitable organizations, signature products, books and regional events. He's won numerous awards and certificates of excellence for his sustainable practices, his partnership with local farmers and producers and the remarkable *taste* of that harmonious food.

"I believe that we have no alternative—there's no Planet B!'" Bob says on his website. "Acting locally with environmentally sustainable business practices is really for our children's children's children (as the Moody Blues album he quotes suggests), from whom we are borrowing this earth."

Values exist whether we recognize them or not

Let me tell you from experience, life can be *so* much easier when we acknowledge, honour and live our values in a deliberate and meaningful way. For example, if you value family but you work eighty hours a week, chances are you're feeling stress, conflict, resentment and imbalance. If you don't value competition and you work in a highly competitive sales environment, how likely are you to be satisfied with your job? If you're teaching your children to do one thing and you're doing the opposite, how much integrity will you have with them or with yourself? Understanding our values is to the foundation of our livelihood. It's the door that can lead to our ability to truly thrive.

Values can be like northern stars helping to guide our every decision. Taking the time to understand our values is a meaningful and foundational exercise. It explains or validates what's truly important to us. It often helps in those situations where we're being "hooked" by someone else's behaviour—when someone is saying or doing something that leads to our over-the-top reaction. It can help give us insight to decipher what's our stuff and what's theirs, what's aligned with our values and what isn't. And this can help facilitate our understanding of those with different values. It can create space for an appreciation of differences and easier interpersonal relationships. It can lead to the ultimate expression of compassion, for ourselves and for others.

When I started working with life coach, Guy Reichard, one of the first things we talked about was my values. Through an academic lens at Seminary, I had learned about the importance of values, but it wasn't until I started the coaching process that I understood how something like a values assessment could really kick start a more meaningful life.

You can find many of these assessments online – I used www.viacharacter.org, which I found very helpful. If you haven't done a values-based exercise like this before, I highly recommend you give it a shot. It asks you a series of multiple-choice questions before generating a twenty-four item list of values based on your answers. It's not the be-all-and-end-all, but it was a good place to start the conversation and begin percolating what felt real, what felt true and what words and meanings caused me to light up inside.

Was it 100% accurate? No. It certainly wasn't a magic bullet. But it did get me thinking about which of those words resonated with me. And at the end of the day, when the kids were in bed and the house was quiet, and the bills were paid and the air was still, it helped me contemplate what mattered most to me. What qualities could I live with, and which could I live without? After talking this through, I ranked my top ten values in priority and then scored my sense of satisfaction—the degree to which I'm honouring each value—using a scale of zero to ten. After giving it time to marinate, I got it down to a list of three core values: Love, Joy and Divinity. Those are my words. Those are my core values. So now I know that when I'm having a bad day, when I'm stressed out and caught up in a moment of doubt or distraction, I can come back to those three words. They're powerful when used regularly and seen and felt often. I've learned that I could call on them when I needed more love or joy or divinity in a situation. I can ask myself, *Is this situation bringing me joy? Is this moment filled with Divine presence? What would 'Love' do or say in this moment?* It has been a real game changer for me. I see it as a blueprint that can help me navigate this life.

Relive a peak moment

After you unearth your own set of core values, you gotta do a peak-moment exercise. The results will seriously light up yer board, ladies. Do me a favour. Sit down, close your eyes, breathe, get quiet and recall a peak moment in time when you felt alive, joyful and free. And I don't mean how it feels to unhook your bra after cooping the girls up all day either (as liberating as that feels). I mean even deeper, like a time when you've had a sense of awe and wonder that stood out from everyday events. Tap into those moments because they can have a lasting effect. After doing this exercise, some people describe having a heightened sense of awareness, fulfillment and spiritual connection. It can happen when you fall in love, when you're in a creative moment, reading a great book or watching a sporting match or movie. Or it can pop up in the most unusual times. Like a funeral. At least that's what happened to me.

After a two-year battle with leiomyosarcoma, a rare cancer, my dear friend, Shelley, died at the age of forty. It happened at a time when we thought things were taking a turn for the better. Treatment had gone well; we thought the road was getting easier. But it all came crashing down one damp February morning. She died in her home in the arms of her mother—the woman who brought her into this world—and surrounded by her husband, step-daughter, father and sister.

When her mother called to tell me the news, everything felt like it was happening in slow motion. Total shock. She shared that it was Shelley's wish for me to speak at her funeral. And so I tried to set aside the confusion and denial so I could write and deliver a eulogy that would truly honour my friend.

Anyone who had known Shelley knew she was like sunshine. At her best, Shelley could illuminate ten New York City blocks. Larger than life, her hair had no choice but to follow suit. That girl had one tremendous set of hair. Just like her, it was electric, far-reaching, stylish and maybe even a little bit wild.

The vibrant colours and daring prints that clung to her classy, sassy curves only accentuated her radiance. To be an item of clothing in that girl's wardrobe! And the accessories! Shelley had some truly outstanding accessories. The purses; the shoes; the bold, bright gemstones that popped off her long, skinny fingers; the stunning, chunky necklaces; the dazzling, dripping earrings that made her mane sparkle even more. She had style, she had groove and grace, and she was simply delicious for all of the senses.

So how was I going to do this? How was I going to write a eulogy about this larger than life person who I couldn't even cry about yet because I was in such a state of shock? And how was I going to say it to a room full of people? And in a Presbyterian Church? Could I swear in a Presbyterian Church? Because honouring Shelley and honouring myself would mean swearing. But I couldn't think of all that at that moment. For the time being, I just needed to collect the stories and write them down.

First I needed to pour myself a glass of wine, actually. And then I needed to sit down and write. And as the Universe would have it, a very vivid flood of memories came through. That was my first peak experience. It's like my mind was playing a movie. I recalled those times when Shelley would show up at the door, walk in the room and just *own* it. You know, one of those kinds of people who can just embody 'tude and girl swagger? She had a sparkle in her eye and a deliberate jiggle in her step. I loved when I'd see her like that. It was so inspiring to me. When the light hit her confidence just right, it was pure energy that everyone wanted to be around. Or at least, the really *fun* people wanted to be around! And if, for some reason, she wasn't right smack in the middle of the room, engineering all the fun, she could be seen in the corner of the room, up to some sort of hilarious mischief.

She was the life of the party! The hub. The disco ball in the heart of the action. She connected people—and connected *with* people. She was like Facebook in the days of Atari.

How was I going to honour someone like this, someone who had been so many things to so many people? How was I going to do it while expressing love, joy and divinity? And then there was the elephant in the room, the distance between us throughout the last five years of her life after she's married her husband whom I came to believe was quite controlling, and I wasn't at a place of resolve with it. So even though it was the woman's funeral, I had to be true. And share my truth. This is when some of my values came through. I had to find the right balance because genuineness is one of my top values too. Even Shelley used to say that I could smell bullshit a mile away. As much as this eulogy was about her, it needed to reflect my values too.

When I got up there to that podium and looked around the jam-packed church, I was nervous as hell. I kept pounding breath mints, like that was somehow going to ease my anxiety. But in that moment, I got this strange feeling that delivering that eulogy was one of my life purposes. Like I was meant to write and speak that eulogy. I felt so compelled to curate memories and her best parts—with truth—and I was going to do it in a way that would make people smile and laugh instead of sobbing and crying. I think that's what she would have wanted. I was going to do it a way that would honour her core values and mine.

And guess what? It worked. I found that sweet spot. I found the vesica piscis! I told stories about her zest and about how much she loved life. I likened her to this big concert hall in our city called the Centre in the Square because she brought so many of us together. I talked about the time we went to see Rita MacNeil's Christmas concert there. Shelley was supposed to go with her beloved grandmother who was under the weather that night and so she asked me to go in her place. What a treat! We had *box seats*, which just felt right or something. And at one point during the concert, somewhere in between "Now the Bells Ring" and "Once Upon a Christmas," Shelley turned to me in all seriousness and said, "Tanya, my box just *belongs* in box seats."

I said this in a Presbyterian Church! I ran this idea past my brother beforehand. He wasn't so sure I should say it. My husband knew it was coming and he sat in a pew bracing himself. I even had second thoughts as the words were rolling off my tongue, but I kept hearing the words in my mind: *Go for it!* I'm not sure if that was her, or me or a Divine force, but first there was a delay, and then the whole church erupted with laughter! Even the minister and funeral director were in stitches. I felt so alive while delivering those words. And truthful and free. It was definitely a peak moment.

It also felt honourable. She wanted people to celebrate her, to laugh at the hundreds of fun times we had all experienced with her. And we did! She wanted us to drink red wine, take a load off, kick off our heels and dance. And we did that too. And she made us promise her there'd be none of those "'effin' funeral sandwiches." I explained to the crowd that she actually dropped a real f-bomb when she said it but my husband, Robert, told me not to say the f-word in a Presbyterian Church. I said that kinda surprised me. Us Lutherans say that sort of shit all the time. The crowd went wild with laughter again! Rolling waves of it. Laughter at a time when you might think we'd be crying. And I knew in that moment that I had both honoured her and I had honoured myself. I had found the sweet spots between both of our value systems.

I wish that everyone reading this could have known Shelley. She has always been such a girl's girl. It's one of the reasons I asked her to be my daughter's godmother. For so many years, you could count on Shelley to be by your side to support you, validate you, bitch with you when you needed it. She also knew when to stop labouring over your troubles and just get out there, with your head held high, buy yourself a nice damn pair of shoes and smile at the sunshine. Get a mani-pedi and be done with it! Empowerment meant so much to Shelley. She even wrote a blog about it for young girls and women of all ages called *Be True*. It was about inspiring, empowering and having conversations with girls to find the community that exists between us.

I tell you all this in a chapter about values because I think it's a good example of how Shelley and I had a different set of values, but we valued each other. And we found that balance between where we found the best in each other, which pulled out the best in other people (in this case their laughter and connectedness). And, at that moment, I found this weird space of feeling so alive at a time when my dear friend was so...*not alive*. But alive and well in spirit. In the words of Maya Angelou, one of Shelley's favourites, "A great soul serves everyone all the time. A great soul never dies. It brings us together again and again."

Recalling peak moments involves getting quiet and still and asking yourself a series of questions, such as, when did you experience a rewarding moment, what was happening, what was going on, who was there, did you feel lit up and what values did you honour in that moment? It offers a way to follow the breadcrumbs back to a time when you felt free and alive—because really, we all want more of that feeling. Living in alignment with your values brings about more of those moments. And recalling those moments not only allows you to experience that joy again, it also offers a path to your values—or helps you validate your list.

Suppressed values

Sometimes it's hard to determine our values because for one reason or another, they've been suppressed for a long time. Another way to isolate values is to go to the opposite extreme, looking at times when you were angry, frustrated, or upset. This often leads to knowing and understanding what value you might have been suppressing. When you can name the feelings and circumstances that led to the upset, you can often flip it over and look for the opposite of those feelings to find your values.

For example, I seem to get angry and upset when people use indirect communication. When Guy was walking me through this exercise, we flipped things around and the answers were there for me. I get triggered because I value transparent communication, genuineness and being direct. Similarly, throughout my career I've sometimes felt trapped, backed into a corner and as though I didn't have choices. But that could stem from the fact that I value options, choice and freedom. There was a period of time when I noticed that several songs on my playlist had the word "freedom" in them and that lit me up inside.

Some people create their lives in a way that automatically honours many of their values without spending too much time focusing on them. They might not recognize them as values until something gets in the way. Upsets or moments of distress are often signals that a value is being suppressed. When it's not a value, it could be a core issue (a thorn, an old wound, an ego defense, etc.). So what's it all lead to? Guy helped me learn that when you honour your values, three amazing things happen:

1. You gain the additional fuel to the motivation fire and help build steam for action,
2. You undermine the work of the Saboteur because action based on values is more powerful than the Saboteur's reasons for not acting or for taking some other course of action and
3. You have a fulfilling life.[8]

Remembering your intrinsic Divine Feminine values

Once you figure out your values, shortlist them to three to put in your toolkit so you can access them at times of need. And remember that you *also* possess the qualities, attributes and values of the Divine Feminine:

1. Wisdom and intuition
2. Unconditional love
3. Compassion
4. Nurturing and helpfulness to others

The Divine Feminine energy of your soul is also comprised of these values. It's powerful energy that allows us to have two-way communication with the Divine and higher realms of consciousness. As women, we are the receptacle—we are the chalice. In fact, the pagan female symbol is called the chalice. It resembles a cup, vessel or womb. We can ask for constant and immediate intuitive guidance, understanding, and knowing on any subject and receive it in our cup. On the flip side, Divine Masculine energy is comprised of:

1. Confidence
2. Strength
3. Courage
4. Willingness to follow Divine guidance (that which is received intuitively through your Divine Feminine energies) and to actively express it and put that Divine guidance into practice in your daily human, outer world life.

We possess this too. Everyone possesses both. Yes, we all have cosmic *man-ginas* and *vag-enises*! But the problem is that often our masculine side is so well developed—sometimes *over*developed—as the sheer result of living in a man's world at this day and age. We need to find the balance, for both women and men. Because when there is harmonic balance between the Divine Feminine and the Divine Masculine, coupled with an understanding of our own personal values that make us unique, we can be healed, freed and whole again.

CHAPTER 2 Reflections:

1. Here's a sample of core values. (There are many more. Do an assessment to narrow yours down and find out more.) Looking at this list, off the top of your head, which five values speak to you most?

Authenticity	Compassion	Curiosity
Achievement	Challenge	Determination
Adventure	Citizenship	Divinity
Authority	Community	Fairness
Autonomy	Competency	Faith
Balance	Contribution	Fame
Beauty	Courage	Friendships
Boldness	Creativity	Fun

Growth	Love	Respect
Happiness	Loyalty	Responsibility
Honesty	Meaningful work	Security
Humour	Openness	Self-respect
Influence	Optimism	Service
Inner harmony	Peace	Spirituality
Joy	Pleasure	Stability
Justice	Poise	Success
Kindness	Popularity	Status
Knowledge	Recognition	Trustworthiness
Leadership	Religion	Wealth
Learning	Reputation	Wisdom

1. Describe a peak moment when you felt totally alive and free. Who was there and what was happening?
2. Describe a time when you were upset, frustrated or angry. What was happening? In that moment, what value(s) do you think you might have been suppressing?
3. Why do you think you're here in this life?

3
Quiet Your Mind and Set Intentions

"Quiet the mind and the soul will speak."
~ MA JAYA SATI BHAGAVATI

"Our intentions create our reality."
~WAYNE DYER

I don't know about you, but my life can be pretty loud. I have young children who are so full of zest, they often sound like they're yelling when they're talking. Our neighbourhood has dog walkers that travel in yelping packs, there's a light rail transit system being built in our city so it's been construction "season" for three years straight. As the seasons change, there's a symphony of snow blowers, lawn mowers and leaf blowers abuzz. I have a landline that rings and cellphones that ding, and even when I do get some quiet time to write, there's instant messaging, Facetime and other social media pop-ups that splat across my computer screen. It can be hard to find a little peace around here!

For years, my internal dialogue would extol the virtues of meditation, and I would find myself thinking, *I should be meditating.* But I spent more time thinking about it than actually doing it, all while "shoulding" all over myself. I also wasn't sure I knew *how* to. I had listened to some guided meditations on YouTube but wasn't sure I was doing it right. I was confused about meditation. Confused by the terms too—did mindfulness and being present mean the same thing? Needless to say, I spent a lot of time talking about meditation instead of practicing it.

That all changed when I started working with Guy. He sold me on the benefits and held me accountable. In a kind, calm and non-judgmental way, he helped me realize that meditation was the kind of stuff I really needed to do in my life. Like really. There was a serious mess that needed to be cleaned up in aisle four and meditation was the mop—my words, not his. So, with the mantra of *what resists, persists* buzzing through my brain, I decided to really give it a try this time. And stick to it.

I realized that I had a mixed-up understanding of what it meant to be present. And what was this flow thing about, really? I thought it was about getting caught up in the moment or not realizing what time it was, like when I was at work creating what felt like my five thousandth strategic communications plan, which I can practically do it in my sleep. For me, it was an unconscious, un-fun exercise in going through the motions and getting it all down on paper and whoops—where did the time go—it's already lunchtime. While flow also relates to an optimal experience, a state of concentration that is so focused that you're completely absorbed, it's different because we also feel strong, alert and at the peak of our abilities—fully connected to an activity, a moment and the Universe. It's a natural, effortless unfolding of our life in a way that moves us toward harmony and wholeness.

But I didn't get that at the time and decided to start meditating anyway despite my confusion. And not a one-and-done either. Like. Every. Single. Day. It has been a huge blessing to me. I feel so much more grounded now, and I'm cranky if I miss a day of meditation (which rarely happens—I even take it with me on vacation). I've folded it into my daily routine. I don't try to find the time; I *make* the time. Like so many, I'm a busy mom with two kids who wake me up before the birds start chirping (and the lawnmowers start going!), so I had to pick something that was going to naturally fit into my lifestyle—and before going off to work at 8:30 a.m. I discovered a website called headspace.com. It has been brilliant for me. In just ten minutes a day, a down-to-earth man named Andy Puddicombe (who's also easy on the eyes, you'll see, when he pops up for the occasional video before a session) with a kind voice and loveable English accent walks me through a ten-minute session (with several series to choose from) that has helped me in more ways than I likely even know. Another great site for guided meditation is fragrantheart.com. Not only did I notice the positive effects of meditation on me, others did too.

In fact, a woman at work who sat in the cubicle next to me turned to me one day and said, "You're doing something different lately, aren't you? And I don't mean your hair. What's going on? What have you been up to?" I told her I was having ravenous sex with my husband, the kind that left me twitching with my eyes rolled back. I'm just kidding. Although that would've certainly cut through the water cooler conversation. But no! The truth was I was meditating on a regular basis! I was delighted she could notice a change. It's like it lowered my baseline and kept worry and upset at bay, levelling me out and keeping me balanced. I don't freak out and despair the way I used to. When I'm meditating regularly, I judge less and my focus strengthens. It's about ten minutes (sometimes fifteen) every day of doing nothing. Simply nothing. Who knew it could give me more energy! And open me up to a world of peace.

Andy has taught me that we need to take time to look after our mind. We spend so much time taking care of our children, our homes, our cars and things at work. And even when it does come to taking care of ourselves, the focus can so easily shift to all the external things: our hair, our nails, our skin and clothes. How often do we take care of our minds? I didn't even know *how* to take care of my mind. It wasn't until I started meditating that I really learned the difference it can make on my brain and the preventative force it can have in my life.

Cultivating wellbeing and happiness starts in your brain

In an article on mindful.org, Richie Davidson, a world-renowned neuroscientist from the Centre for Healthy Minds at the University of Wisconsin-Madison, shares three important pieces of information about mindfulness:

1. You can train your brain to change,
2. Change is measurable and
3. New ways of thinking can change it for the better.[9]

He likens it to a skill, like learning how to play the piano. The results stopped me in my tracks. Did you know that we could influence the plasticity of our brains—and shape them in ways that can be beneficial—by focusing on wholesome thoughts and directing our intentions in those ways? So much so that it shows up on brain scans? This is about increasing grey matter, people! And cortical thickness (that's a good thing)! Here's where and how meditation is showing up and helping our brains. Increased grey matter changes were noted in the:

- **Anterior Cingulate Cortex (ACC)-** A structure located behind the frontal lobe, the ACC is associated with self-regulatory processes, including the ability to monitor attention conflicts and allow for more cognitive flexibility.
- **Prefrontal Cortex:** The prefrontal cortex is the area of the prefrontal lobe that is primarily responsible for planning, problem solving and emotion regulation.

And meditation increases cortical thickness in the:

- **Hippocampus:** The hippocampus is the part of the limbic system that governs learning and memory. It's extraordinarily susceptible to stress and stress-related disorders such as depression and PTSD.[10]

After a mindfulness practice, studies have shown a decrease in the size of the amygdala, which is known as our brain's fight-or-flight centre and the place of our fearful and anxious emotions. Not only does the amygdala shrink after a mindfulness practice, the functional connections between the amygdala and the prefrontal cortex are also weakened, which allows for less reactivity. It paves the way for connections to be strengthened between areas associated with higher order brain functions such as attention and concentration.

Finally—and possibly most beautifully—the practice of mindfulness has been connected with decreased activation and stilling of our Default Mode Network (DMN), sometimes referred to as our wandering "monkey minds." The DMN is active when our minds are directionless and go from thought to thought, a response that is sometimes likened to rumination and not always adaptive. This can impede overall happiness.

The effect mindfulness has on our brains is amazing. And it comes from a simple routine: a slow, steady, and consistent reckoning of our realities and the ability to take a step back, become more aware, more accepting, less judgmental, and less reactive.

We spend so little time in the present moment. In 2010, the *Harvard Gazette* published a study about how 47% of our waking hours were spent thinking about what *isn't* going on.[11] In other words, we're thinking about something other than what we're doing, and all this mind wandering is making us unhappy.

The research was conducted by psychologists Matthew A. Killingsworth and Daniel T. Gilbert of Harvard University, and in the report they said "the ability to think about what is not happening is a cognitive achievement that comes at an emotional cost."[12]

Humans are unique among animals in this way. We spend a lot of time thinking about what isn't going on around us and contemplating events that happened in the past, events that might—or might not—even happen in the future. Mind wandering appears to be the human brain's default mode of operation.

That just makes me sad. And it reminds me of a Francis Bacon quote I recently came across: "Begin doing what you want to do now. We are not living in eternity. We have only this moment, sparkling like a star in our hand—and melting like a snowflake..." It's so true. We *don't* have eternity—anyone who has lost a loved one who died too young knows it. We only have the here and now. We only have this moment. I believe that a moment in full presence is like experiencing eternity—beyond the limits of time and space. And I want to spend more time there. Here. Right now. I want to spend more time feeling my fingers bounce off this keyboard. I want to spend more time connecting with you through my writing and my words. I want to spend more time feeling love and fullness and abundance of all that is here and living and thriving and dancing with me right now—the light streaming in the windows, clean air filling my lungs, the symphony of my household.

I want to bask in this jubilee of life around me. It starts by living and truly saturating ourselves in the living, present and vibrating moment. It starts with getting quiet and disconnecting from our phones and connecting to the Divine and all other living things. It starts with stillness and meditation and reverence for life and all that is right here and right now. It is about being witness to The Great I Am. And it only takes ten minutes a day—longer if you have it but even ten minutes will do. The return is rich and meaningful with benefits for you and others around you.

Getting down with nature

Another way to get into flow with the Universe is to invoke Mother Earth herself. Have you ever tried it? I thought the whole tree hugging kind of thing wasn't really for me and that was validated when I came across an article giving instructions on how to befriend a tree. I admit to jumping to some pretty snickery judgments about it and thought it might work for some people, but not this sister. *I'm far too Type A for this exercise*, I thought to myself. As if befriending a tree would do anything other than make me look like a total buffoon in front of my suburban neighbours! But then...I tried it.

I was at a Prince Edward Island cottage on the edge of the Atlantic Ocean. One afternoon, after a couple of glasses of pinot grigio, while my husband and kids were down playing on the red-sand beach, I mustered up the (liquid) courage to try this nature-connecting thing out. So up in front of the cottage, I laid face down on the green earth, under a tree, and breathed deeply holding the intention of just being. After all, we are human beings, not human doings. I had to keep repeating to myself to stay in that moment: *Just be. Be. Breathe in, breathe out and be.*

It was excruciatingly uncomfortable at first. The grass was too itchy and I thought I might be allergic. I thought about the gasoline it took to mow the lawn that morning and was I breathing it in? What if I swallowed a bug? Were there worms in this grass? This couldn't be good for me. Itch, itch, itch. But, after a period of resistance, I let go. And there was peace. Silence. Stillness. Boredom. And then the unexpected: tears. For the first time in months, I did nothing but cry. And under a tree.

The tears came slow and steady, and I didn't understand why they were there or what they were about, but they came, and it took great focus and intention on accepting this experience, as it was, and as a gift. I didn't know why I was doing this or what made me cry, but I came to the conclusion that I didn't need to know. I just needed to accept that it was happening, accept that the tears were real and wet. I didn't need to know why and it was okay. A wise woman once told me that tears are a way of washing the soul, and I didn't have to explain or defend them. I realized then that I needed to experience this more often—and for the sum of its benefits, maybe even at home in front of the neighbours. After all, they watched my family, with adoration and encouragement, grow and tend to a vegetable garden at the side of our property. Maybe they'd be receptive to this sort of wild and wonderful activity too. And even if they weren't, it would be okay. I wouldn't die or be evicted from my home.

What's the worst that could happen? Someone might judge me? Or maybe, just maybe, I'd inspire courage within them to do something like this to connect with nature and set intentions too. And just be. One with nature, one with Mother Earth, Father Time and...one with The Universe. Our ancestors knew and understood this emotional connection with their physical surroundings, and they were engaged in continuous conversation with Mother Nature. Why aren't we?

Watch your words

Marianne Williamson, spiritual teacher, author and world-renowned speaker once said: "You must learn a new way to think before you can master a new way to be." And it all starts with words. Language shapes our behaviour, and each word we use is infused with masses of personal meanings. The right words, spoken in the right way, can bring us love, money and respect, while the wrong words—or even the right words spoken in the wrong way—can lead a country to war.[13] Words are powerful. They are like offerings that become intentions and prayers waiting to be answered. The Old Testament revealed that. In Genesis, it says that: "In the beginning was the Word. And the word was God and the word was with God."[14]

Famous poet, author and director, the late Maya Angelou, knew the power of words. She said: "Words are things. You must be careful, careful about calling people out of their names, using racial pejoratives and sexual pejoratives and all that ignorance. Don't do that. Some day we'll be able to measure the power of words. I think they are *things*. They get on the walls. They get in your wallpaper. They get in your rugs, in your upholstery, and your clothes, and finally into *you*."

We must be careful with the words we use—not just when describing situations or others, but when describing ourselves. Because as Mahatma Gandhi suggested in his quote mentioned in the last chapter, our words, thoughts and beliefs are interconnected, as are our actions. Knowing this was true, recently I had to step in and protect my daughter because I didn't want the words of one of her teachers to have an effect on her beliefs and ultimately who she is. It's a story I even struggle to tell right now because it still has left me feeling hot-angry. But there was resolve, and so I'll share it. I hope it serves as inspiration to others.

The other b-word

So, my daughter was five years old and in senior kindergarten when she came home one day with her report card in her backpack. Now, when it comes to report cards, my husband and I have decided to a) not make a big deal of them, b) read what the teachers have to say but not treat it as gospel—we know our kids and c) not even discuss this whole report card phenomenon with our kids until they reach an age when they actually *ask* about it. Life's already too full of evaluations and scorecards. We decided to postpone this as long as possible. And even when our kids do ask, we'll revisit a) and not make a big deal of it.

Because the way I see it, that's one person's (or maybe two people's) observation of how our kids are doing a few hours a day while observing what twenty-some-odd other kids are doing and while teaching lessons and running through the daily routine. So, I listen to the feedback from a place of curiosity to understand what they're observing when I'm not around. And because you can't be curious and in judgment at the same time—our brains won't allow it—I chose to be curious.

Until I read the first two sentences of her English report card (she attends a bilingual school so she had one report in English and the other in French), which read: "Georgia had a good second term. She is a cooperative and friendly student, but on occasion she tends to be bossy with her friends, which leads to conflicts."

The rest of the report was glowing, but I reeled over that second sentence because of that word—*Bossy*!

What does it mean and why do we use it? Being a woman of words, I did what felt natural. I looked it up. The Canadian Oxford dictionary says the word *bossy* means 'fond of giving people orders; domineering: e.g. *don't be so bossy! a bossy, meddling woman.*[15]' Even the freakin' Canadian Oxford dictionary attributes it to women.

Now let me ask this: how many boys you know have been called *bossy*? Typically, when a man (or boy) says what he wants and takes action, he's called *assertive*, which the same dictionary defines as 'having or showing a confident and forceful personality: e.g. The job may call for assertive behaviour.'[16]

Bossy is a put-down and a word typically associated with females, and assertive is a compliment, which is more often associated with males. And we wonder why women—who make up 51% of both the Canadian and American populations—only make up just *5.3%* of Canadian CEOs, and in 2013, held just 15.9% of board seats in S&P/TSX 60 companies. And in the United States, women hold a paltry 4.2% of CEO positions in America's 500 biggest companies.[17] There is a real problem here.

I worked with a remarkable leader, Isabelle Hudon — now Canada's Ambassador to France — who was passionate about this topic. She has been a part of many boards throughout her career. In fact, the Quebec government once asked her to join a special committee that was examining diversity within boards. Isabelle has been courageously frank about this topic. "Let me tell you," she said in a *Canadian Business Magazine* interview, "when you get on the phone to try to convince a woman to take a seat on a board, you have to take a vitamin and make sure you're feeling great, because the *questions* you have to go through! 'Am I good enough? Will I be welcomed? Why do they want me?' Yet you call a guy and he says, 'OK. What time? Where?'"[18]

This made me even more curious about where this lack of self-confidence originated from and if it most often traced back to childhood? Like to senior-fucking-kindergarten, for example. And then I stopped being curious and started being hopping angry—which I let myself do for a while, knowing I had to get myself in check before the parent-teacher interview that week.

Now I do admit to the fact that I was also listening to a lot of Meghan Trainor at the time (love that girl) and so my Divine Feminine sass, self-love and womanly love was frothing up and spilling out all over the place. And while it's true that the teacher who wrote the "bossy" comment was gone by then, I still needed to address it. Because even if the woman who wrote it was gone, someone had to type the thing out and other people had to sign it. This was an official record that had been seen by more than one person and this shit wasn't getting past me. Words. They're powerful! So I calmly and *ASSERTIVELY* voiced my experience in reading those words on my five-year-old child's report card. I stressed that if Georgia was trying to suggest to others that they couldn't have their own creative opinion when they were playing with her, or trying to control the situation beyond what was appropriate, I was open to hearing that and glad to speak with her about it. But I also said I was taken aback by reading that word. I saw it as a label, a put-down, and now that Georgia could read, I wouldn't let her see that report card because I didn't want her to see the words that her teacher (whom she looked up to and admired tremendously) had said about her and for her to internalize it or worse, *believe* it.

No child of mine would be dimming her lamp to satisfy what one woman considered a social norm—for one gender anyway. Not on my watch.

While I tempered self-righteousness in that moment, I was also proud of myself. Georgia's teachers listened to me and I felt that they heard what I was saying. That was enough for me. I felt good. I would continue mothering Georgia and encouraging her to use her voice, speak out, say what she wants, own her feelings—be big and strong and powerful if that is what she was feeling. I was her advocate and I couldn't care less how I was viewed. But what shocked me was what happened next.

A few days later, my husband came home from picking up the kids and, with a smile on his face, handed me a long brown envelope. It was from Georgia's teacher. I opened it up and saw that it was another copy of Georgia's report card except this one had been changed. The second sentence didn't read that Georgia was bossy; it has been changed to assertive. The rest of it was the same. The teacher told Robert she listened to what I said and agreed with me, and quite honestly hadn't read what the English supply teacher had written. So she asked the office to change it and she wanted me to have a copy.

I love when things like that happen. A negative turns into a positive and not only does goodness prevail but connections are formed. There was a glimmer in the teacher's eye the next time I saw her. She knows. She gets it—she has daughters too. We made a connection; we became Warrior Women together and we're doing good for our girls coming up the path.

Words are powerful. We need to choose them wisely all the while remembering our divinity. Would an angel speak that way? Would God speak that way? Would we reflect the Divine Mother if speaking that way? Because we are all Divine beings. We were called into being by the life source of love and hope and goodness and we must uphold, honour and teach that. Teach it to our children. Teach it to the world. Teach it by living it ourselves and modelling the way. That's integrity. That's alignment with intentions, words and actions. That's One-ness. And that's being alive and well in this moment. That is truth and light and all good things. It's available to us every second of the day. And that alone is freedom.

The power of intentions: Lao Tzu, Dr. Wayne Dyer and Hafiz wisdom

We have the freedom to choose how we are going to live our lives, what we are going to teach our children, how we are going to leave this planet better off. And it starts with silence, intentions and words. The book *Hua Hu Ching*, the unknown teachings of Lao Tzu, alludes to the power of intentions. Number 51 says:

> "Those who want to know the truth of the universe should practice the four cardinal virtues. The first is reverence for all of life. This manifests as unconditional

love and respect for oneself and all other beings. The second is natural sincerity. This manifests as honesty, simplicity and faithfulness. The third is gentleness, which manifests as kindness, consideration for others and sensitivity to spiritual truth. The fourth is supportiveness. This manifests as service to others without expectation of reward.[19]"

In a 2008 *Successful Living* article that featured an interview with inspirational speaker and best-selling author, the late Dr. Wayne Dyer, he calls out that the great spiritual masters have been teaching the same principles for centuries: forgiveness, love, kindness. "They aren't teaching about wanting or greed or when the Universe is going to put a BMW in the driveway. It's not about wanting more and having more and becoming more. That's not the power of intention; that's the ego's mantra of "What's in it for me? How can I get more?" That's the false self, the ego."[20]

According to Dyer, the process of allowing, just being and embracing this heightened level of consciousness, goes back not to attracting what you want but attracting what you are. "You have to just be. You have to let go. You have to allow. You have to be free and make this your consciousness." He continues, "Basically, what you would see is a frequency (of energy) that manifests itself through the process of giving, of allowing, of offering and of serving. It asks nothing back."[21] The concept of giving without expectations is illustrated by this quote by the great poet Hafiz: "Even after all this time, the sun never says to the earth 'you owe me.'"[22]

Intentions, like all other forms of thoughts, are waves that silently ripple, expanding out from the mind and into the Universe.[23]

- Make a consistent practice of getting quiet through meditation.
- Understand the power and importance of words.
- Have intentions and remember them often. Make them honourable and not just self-serving. Use them for good and to help others. Activate them through the calm of prayer or meditation.
- Stay grounded in reverence for life, sincerity, gentleness and supportiveness.
- And watch as the Universe conspires in your favour.

CHAPTER 3 Reflections:

1. What steps do you take to quiet your mind?
2. How do you connect with nature? How does it connect back with you?
3. Have you ever had a moment in nature when it deeply moved you or gave you a sense of something, a wisdom of sorts? What did you learn?
4. How mindful are you with your words?
5. Do you recall a time when someone used powerful words toward you, and how did it affect you?
6. How do you feel about the word "bossy?"

4
Heal Your Mother Wounds

"You can accept or reject the way you are treated by other people, but until you heal the wounds of your past, you will continue to bleed. You can bandage the bleeding with food, with alcohol, with drugs, with work, with cigarettes, with sex, but eventually, it will all ooze through and stain your life. You must find the strength to open the wounds, stick your hands inside, pull out the core of the pain that is holding you in your past, the memories, and make peace with them."

~ IYANLA VANZANT, *YESTERDAY, I CRIED*

Acknowledging your divinity, understanding your values, getting quiet and intentional are all very important, but before you move onto really living the life you were meant to live—really moving in the direction of your soul—you need to remove any boulders that might be standing in your way. That has been my experience anyway. And let me tell you, those boulders, they can be heavy. So here's where it's time to put on our sweats, roll up our sleeves and do some work. I'm talking about soul work here. Like therapy, life coaching, energy work. I'm talking about doing just what Iyanla described in her quote—reaching into our wounds and pulling out the core pain from the past and then basting them with spiritual salve and making healing peace with it. Accepting the scars into the unique tapestry of our skin. Before we move on, we need to love them for helping make us who we are and being a part of our story. And as much as I love and advocate for living in the present, sometimes we need to look back first—for a limited period of time anyway—before we can truly be still, acknowledge the past, be at peace and move onto finding joy in the present.

Until we work through the pain found in old wounds (often with professional help), it'll just keep coming up. Like a beach ball we just keep trying to stuff underwater, at some point that thing's going to pop up again, often in places we don't want or expect. Have you ever had this happen before?

When my husband and I were dating, his grandfather died a month before my grandfather did. Robert gave the eulogy at his grandfather's funeral, and I remember my stoic father-in-law being proud of him for not crying or "showing too much emotion." (Massive eye roll.) When we found ourselves in a funeral home a month later, mourning the death of my grandfather this time, it was like Robert cracked wide open, and all of the grief that he held together to get through the death of his grandfather and his eulogy rose to the surface. He barely knew my grandfather, but his grief for his own loss resisted the pressure of being stuffed down any longer.

Having the courage to face and heal the injuries of our soul can open up a world we couldn't even imagine possible before having worked through it—a more authentic, genuine life that helps us see with clearer eyes and a clearer heart. This was true for one of my dear friends. On the eve of her sixtieth birthday, Anne,* a remarkable woman, had two profound realizations. The first was that in all of her years, she had yet to truly experience what it was to feel desire. The second realization was that she was now finally getting a taste of it—except it was for another woman.

Looking back to step forward

Anne had a painful childhood. She was sexually abused by her father while trying to manage her mother, who knew but turned a blind and jealous eye. Anne was also trying to protect her younger sisters from experiencing the same horror. She finally found relief, escape and even happiness in her early twenties when she married her husband and started a family. Life was busy with work and family and when her husband was struck with a sudden cancer diagnosis in his early forties, it shook them to their cores. His illness was sudden and in a few short months he died leaving Anne to raise their two pre-adolescent boys. Alone. Anne says she spent most of the next twenty years grieving, rebuilding her life and helping her sons cope with the loss of their father. Therapy sessions happened at regular intervals and helped her work through the pain of her past so she could open herself up to the present and future.

Eventually, Anne decided she wanted to find love again. She tried dating a few men, but after trial and error over a period of time, she resigned herself to the fact that maybe dating wasn't for her, and being on her own would make her happier. She thought she didn't *need* to be in a relationship to live a fulfilling life. In fact, she joked about it with her friend, Christine.*

---

* Names changed to protect privacy.

Christine had been through her own difficult childhood marked with sexual abuse. She found comfort in not only therapy but on a path to becoming a therapist herself. Christine was attracted to women. She wasn't in a relationship either and often felt quite lonely, having strained family ties because of her past. Anne and Christine became fast friends and agreed to build their own 'framily' (friends who are like family) and support each other through single life and older age.

But Anne started having what she described as "strange feelings" toward Christine. After a lot of soul searching and bewilderment, she realized it was in fact a *crush*. This all came to a head the day before her sixtieth birthday. Anne paced the room about it, having this internal conflict and realizing that this might be what desire actually feels like. And wow, she had never truly experienced it before! The timing was also a surprise. Anne had just taken a pause from years of therapy, feeling as though she was in a good solid place now where she had made peace with her past, rewrote her story and could take it from here. (When one door closes, another opens.) After stewing about it in her house for a while, Anne decided to take a walk and ask God for a sign to help her understand these feelings. Was it a crush? Was she a lesbian too? "Give me a sign," she asked, "God, please give me a sign that I can recognize so I'll know what to do."

The next day, two of her girlfriends came over to wish her a happy birthday. Knowing her love of gardening, they brought her a gift to place in her flowerbed—a giant cast-iron beaver. Anne took one look at it and burst out laughing, recognizing that not only was the Divine communicating with her and giving her the answers she needed, but God also had a sense of humour! She recognized this as the divine go-ahead to explore her own beaver (and maybe somebody else's!) and find the happiness and desire unlike she had ever experienced before. Anne's story is a reminder that at sixty, eighty or even one hundred and four, it's never too late. And it's up to us to do the work and author our own stories so we can be ready to receive the next gift.

Over the years, Anne and I have talked a lot about healing what she calls our "mother wounds," that karmic knot of physical and emotional trauma that many of us need to heal. It's not a process that can be rushed through quickly. Even now that her mother is gone, it's a topic we still revisit often. A mother wound cuts deep; it damages the body-mind, needs its due healing and often scars the body or emotional composition. It's a primal relationship. Your mother, or the person who mothered you (or didn't mother you well enough) affects your development on a cellular level and conditions much of your life. Just because you grow up doesn't mean you've resolved these feelings. I remember talking with a friend who kept encountering what she described as "cold and controlling women" in her life. They were like that "Whac-a-Mole" game at a carnival—as soon as she hammered one of them down, another would pop up. But it's because she hadn't dealt with her mother fully, the one who was at the end of that string of women. She hadn't patiently sat through the rage and discomfort and sadness. It may seem terribly inefficient to do this – especially for multi-taskers of the world – but it's so necessary. By not acknowledging and making peace with those feelings, she was forced to stay caught in her heart and mind with this negative mother image that prevented the possibility of an authentic relationship. She was too afraid of getting hurt or being rejected. But there is a mindfulness practice to move past this entanglement. It's not a magic bullet. It takes time and healing but it works. It's called visioning backwards.

Rewriting *her*story

In Western culture, we talk a lot about having a vision. What's your vision? Where do you want to be five years from now? It's future oriented and often feels unachievable. While stretching ourselves and having aspirations have their merits, unless we've healed what's behind us, it's almost impossible to go the distance. We need a strong foundation to build on. And more often than not, after healing past wounds, our vision changes from what it once was to become something different. Visioning backward can provide a more authentic roadmap. Unless we've cleansed old wounds and re-written our history (*her*story?) in a way that those events are now part of our story—having strengthened us along the way—how can we have clarity and the peace to truly move on?

What I wish more people—individuals, families, corporations, churches, school boards, governments, you name it—would do is a visioning backwards exercise because it's one way to heal our wounds and make our future vision seem more exciting and achievable. Healing, owning and retelling our stories in a way that past events become folded into our lives without judgment, hurt or blame. It allows us to overcome a sense of being a victim of them. It gives way to an acknowledgement of the people and events that have influenced our lives and compels us to focus on the right things instead of giving all that power to the pain and what was underneath. It helps us get our needs met in a much more direct, authentic and healing way.

Here's how you do it: you rewrite your story. Now you might be wondering how on earth do we do that, especially when we tell ourselves stories to live, exist and make sense of this world. In her 1979 book of essays, *The White Album*, Joan Didion described living by "the imposition of a narrative line, upon disparate images" because of a critical need to "freeze the shifting phantasmagoria which is our actual experience."[24] I had to look up what phantasmagoria means, which the Oxford Dictionary defines as "a sequence of real or imaginary images like that seen in a dream."[25] And think about what happens when you're dreaming or better yet, having a nightmare. You're telling yourself a story that is outside of waking reality and your body reacts. You start tossing and turning, your heart begins racing or you start sweating because your body can't tell the difference between what is real and what is imagined. If this is true then why can't we reprogram our past to make it easier to digest and move on, past something as debilitating as a mother wound?

It can take the form of meditation, journal writing or conversation (try recording it to reflect on your evolution later). Recount the facts of your childhood or past loves without any embellishments and then express gratitude for all of it—even the tough parts—because you made it through. First retell your story as though you're a victim. You're cold and controlling because of your mother. You judge people harshly because your father judged you harshly. You don't trust people because of your ex-boyfriend. Or you have a man who seems to be right but you still find things wrong with him. Then retell the story without blaming someone. Will you still have a story to tell?

Rewrite your story in a way that layers factual events into your story with a different perspective. We tend to easily recall a story a little differently than the way it actually happened. There are many different angles to a situation. Why not rewrite your story in a way that empowers you when you remember it? Try putting a positive spin on negative events in an effort to embrace happiness or a deeper sense of ease from recalling your past.

Patchwork mother

Because the mother-child relationship is the foundation of our development, it's important to note that even if you didn't get the mothering you needed, you can turn to find the mothering you long for in fragments within your circle of support. Even as an adult. It might look like patchwork—you might be going to your favourite aunt for comfort and validation, your mentor for career direction, your neighbour to help you fix something or an older sister to build you up when you're down—but it works. And quilts are beautiful.

My healing came back to a place of deep inner longing to be mothered in a different way than what I experienced with my earthly mother. I love my mother. She's a wonderful nana and our relationship has never been better. All of the ways that I experienced her have led me to being the person I am today. But growing up, it wasn't always easy, and I longed to be mothered on a deeper level. And so did she. Growing up, my mother was left to fend for herself most of the time and care for her younger siblings in a damp flat in England. Her mother didn't give my mother what she needed physically, emotionally and certainly not spiritually, which is what so many of us long for without even really being able to identify it.

Longing for Divine Mother

For years, I too have struggled with this deep, longing desire to be mothered, which I've beat myself up about because I'm forty-two years old and *hello,* I am a mother myself. Why do I need to be mothered when I am a mother? And it's hard to focus on that while I have little ones pulling at my shirt to get them something else. But it's worth going back and healing, not only for myself but also so that I can be a better mother to them. I admit, there's still some shame around it.

What I've realized is that it goes much deeper than ties with the mother I have been raised by in this human lifetime. It goes back to mother source—the sacred energy of a mother. A Divine Mother. That is what I have been truly longing for, and for the longest time, I felt like I couldn't find her. Where was she? Why had she been stripped out of religious text, scriptures and literature? Where was my Divine Mother? Why couldn't I find her? I needed her, and I was longing for her. I needed to feel her presence and loving arms around me, protecting me always. And only recently did a little light creep in on that hope. Only recently did I discover that maybe it's normal and valid to want this energy-force in my life. And maybe there are others who long for her too. Maybe she doesn't even need to be a person. Maybe there's a deeper spiritual longing for a mother that deeply satisfies my soul. And maybe she's already within me.

This prompted further research on the Divine Feminine and what I felt was missing from my spiritual teachings. I want to be loved by her and truly seen by her, recognized as her beloved, cherished daughter. I want to be comforted and pampered by her. I want it to be all about me for once. And to feel like she's always right by my side even when I think she isn't. I want to stop feeling sad about missing her or feeling forsaken in my deep desire to be mothered. I want to know with a deep, wise knowing that she is here and all is well and I can sleep soundly at night.

I think my relationship with God would have deepened and strengthened sooner if I felt like I could have related more to Him. If He was also a She. And so today, I see my Heavenly Father as my Heavenly Parents. And I dropped the guilt of feeling disrespectful for independently (and without permission) changing God's gender. Because seriously, how can we honestly say, in full confidence, that we know the gender of a God that isn't human? God is God. And even the word God is difficult for me to relate to sometimes. The word can sound stark, distant and not soft. I like the Hebrew word for God better, *Yahweh*. It sounds like breathing when you say it—like breath. You can't close your lips around it or contain it within your mouth like the word God. Yahweh flows. It's a pretty word, and it captures more of the Divine Mother essence to me.

It might sound a bit like the start of an AA class, but I had to come to accept that: I'm Tanya Sood. I'm forty-two years old. And I want to be mothered. By my Divine and most holy loving Mother. And I want to know that she recognizes me and sees me and knows me and is so in awe of me. I want to feel special to her, like her one and only daughter. And I want all women to feel this way around her too. Everyone—women and men—deserve this Divine Mothering.

And so that's what this journey is really all about for me, reuniting me with my Divine Mother, the Mother who loves me unconditionally, the Mother who thinks I am beautiful and kind and precious and she's so proud of me. And she can't wait to show me things and teach me things and she's giddy when I come to visit. She's alive and thrilling and exciting, and I am inspired and comforted by her. And she thinks I'm just incredible and wants to hear all about me and comfort me at every opportunity. She wants to care for me and love me and honour me and teach me and inspire me and see the greatness in me. She's my biggest supporter, and she pulls me up when I feel like I have nothing left. And she makes me tea and draws me a bath with Epsom salts and just the right essential oils to cure whatever ails me. And she wraps me in a fluffy robe after, brushes my hair, paints my nails red and cloaks me with her love. You know, the Mother-of-all-Mothers kinda mothering.

Into the arms of the Divine Mother

Recently, I attended a weekend workshop in Maine, hosted by author, speaker and life coach, Cheryl Richardson. "Self-care by the Sea" was a truly amazing experience. I'm still in awe of how much I learned in one weekend! We talked a lot about mothering during this session. We talked about the Divine Feminine. Meggan Watterson, author of *Reveal: A Sacred Manual for Getting Spiritually Naked* was there too. And there was an exercise that Meggan walked us all through—a guided meditation and visualization. She asked us to imagine a set of stairs in front of us that led up to a door. What I saw and experienced in that moment was unlike any other visualization I had ever experienced before. It was so vivid, so technicolour, so RED, the colour of the Divine Feminine. It blew me away.

So when I got to the top of the steps, I walked in and there was my Divine Mother, who had long flowing white hair and a beautiful golden aura around her. She had been waiting for me with the same longing I had for her. She wanted to hug, kiss and hold me in her arms and cherish me. And so she did. I allowed her to and it felt so nice. She told me how much she loved me and had missed me, and we held each other for what seemed like a long time. And then she took my hand and led me into another room of this castle of sorts, and she put a golden staff in my hand and a crown on my head. And I sat on a throne beside her. There were all these people in front of me, and they kept whispering something about it being coronation day (for a moment I questioned myself for watching *Frozen*[26] too many times with my six-year-old daughter but tried to snuff out the judgments and just stick with it). And then I walked out to a balcony to address the people. It felt like a scene from *Evita*.[27] Except when I looked down, I realized they weren't people. First I thought they were drones or something flying around my head, but then I realized they were butterflies. Before I knew it, I was transported to a field and there were beautiful, colourful butterflies flying all around me. For a moment, I looked around and was heartbroken because I thought my Divine Mother had left me, but there she was, standing right behind me. Always there.

I hadn't experienced such a vivid visualization before. So what did it all mean? Well, I think first and foremost, visualization exercises can be powerful, especially when you do them with other people and say a little intention in the beginning for everyone to receive the messages they most need to hear at that moment. Second, that night a thought came to me that added another smile to my face. My parents named me Tanya, a name that means 'queen.' (Check out the meaning of your name at a site such as www.babycenter.ca/baby-names-finder.) When my Divine Mother put the crown on my head, it was like she was crowning me or giving me permission to be myself. It was coronation day and I was being crowned as the true Divine me. It was a powerful exercise and later I stumbled upon a James Baldwin quote that summed up the experience beautifully for me: "Your crown has already been bought and paid for. All you must do is put it on."

That's all I needed to do.

Try doing a similar exercise for yourself. Close your eyes, breathe in deeply through your nose and out of your mouth for equal counts (I count to four), and think of yourself in a beautiful, natural place. It could be a meadow or a forest with vibrant colours and meandering wildlife. Keep walking until you come across a clearing and a path that you see will lead you to a beautiful castle in the distance. Walk the path, knowing it was meant just for you, until you reach the front door. Notice its beauty. Turn the handle, push the door open, hear its sound and walk inside to a most welcoming entranceway adorned just for your arrival. Notice a set of double doors ahead of you. Walk toward them and let yourself into the room, set up like a study. You're surprised to see that there, at a long desk, sits a wise person—living or dead—whom you revere and most admire. They are delighted to see you. Imagine that they have a large book on the desk in front of them. They smile and signal you to come over to sit on the chair beside them. After you sit down, they take your hand to show you the passage of the book that is specifically intended for you to read.

It starts with a word. See it in your mind. Beside it is a description of the word's meaning and an explanation of why you need to see and know and breathe that word into your life right now. It is a teacher. It is teaching you on behalf of the Universe. What do you need to know about that word? Drink it in. Smile with a knowingness, awareness and acceptance of it. Only after this will you be shown what to do with this information. Thank the wise person at the desk in a way that is most fitting to you. Leave the study, move through the entrance way and out the door knowing that the full meaning of this word is now unfolding in your life and will show you the way. Recall it often. This is how you dance with grace.

Another powerful exercise we did on that retreat that you might want to try at home is that we wrote a list of ten to twelve things we wished our mothers had of said to us. Then we had to find a partner (i.e. a total stranger) and sit on chairs facing each other, knees touching, and pretend that the woman sitting in front of us was our mother. We had to say each item on the list to her and she would repeat it back to us as though she was our mother, and saying it with love, kindness and conviction. Nice, huh?

I was a blubbering fucking mess. And I didn't even go first! I played the mother figure for my partner first, and I could barely sputter out the words for her. I was a hot holy mess by the time it was my turn! And the clincher—once we finished our list of twelve, we had to start at the beginning and say it all over again. Multiple times. Until we heard the bell chimes. It was agony at first but eventually more soothing than I could imagine. A very powerful exercise. A freeing exercise. I highly recommend it. And I liked that we were asked to write the list first because it was very intimate, and I had no idea I'd be sharing it with another person, let alone a stranger. We convened afterward and shared some of the things we longed to hear. Here are some of the things I heard from the group. I hope will inspire you when creating your own list:

1. You are scathingly brilliant—wicked smart.
2. You are so beautiful and kind-hearted.
3. I believe in you and you can be and do anything.
4. You are safe with me; your heart is safe with me. I will hold you and protect you, your heart and your dreams.
5. You amaze me. You take my breath away.
6. I don't know what I did to deserve being your mother—it's my greatest gift.
7. You are on fire with passion and love and girl, you are going places!
8. I see you and you matter so much to me.
9. You were a dream of mine that came true—exceeding my wildest hopes. I wanted you. You're a gift in my life.
10. You are pure love and I honour you.
11. I want you to be powerful.
12. I will never intentionally hurt you.

Into the lap of the Divine Mother

Recently, I was doing a different guided meditation than I typically do. It's called "Into the Lap of the Divine Mother" by Kathleen McIntire.[28] It's a beautiful eight-minute escape that

I found online, and it gave me lots of Divine Mother energy return at a time when I really needed it. In this meditation, Kathleen walks you through an exercise of finding your way to sit upon your Divine Mother's lap. And there you can experience all of this unconditional love—a heart bursts open with it. And you realize that you're perfect just the way you are, and there's nothing you need to do or change because you are deeply loved for just being yourself.

The biggest thing I took from that exercise was toward the end when the Divine Mother says, "If there's anything you'd like to talk to me about—any concerns or problems you're facing—please tell me right now." And then Kathleen asks us to listen quietly for she has an answer. She has words of wisdom that the Divine Mother wants to give us at this very moment. Silence. The Divine Mother says to find quiet time to listen to your intuition. She always speaks through us if we find time to be quiet and to listen. She's always with us, here to guide us.

As tears streamed down my face, I was instantly reminded of my human mothering experience with my children and in particular, with my son. Everett is such a bright, smart, amazing little boy. He's eight now and has stout curiosity about almost all things that stretch across this universe and beyond (and especially hockey and baseball facts). He likes to talk. And talk and talk and talk, and I don't want to interrupt him sometimes because I see all this energy and his thought processes and his mind just going. But sometimes I want him to be quiet long enough for him to listen to me. Because I, too, want to hold him in my arms or tuck him into bed and tell him just how precious and beautiful and wonderful he is to me and to this world. But to hear me say those words, he needs to be quiet. And for me to hear the Divine Mother's words, I need to be quiet too. She is the marvellous life force and she wants to be recognized and heard within our souls.

She is our intuition. She is our wisdom. The magnitude of her tenacity comes to those who are brave enough to trust her and allow her to erect a big centre pole in the tent of our souls. She'll help us to rise up and meet our highest, greatest, most robust and multi-dimensional selves. When our energy field shifts this way, our consciousness expands, our nervous system neutralizes, and we begin to fully realize and experience a spiritual awakening. With the recognition of our Divine essence, things become possible that weren't before. Fears diminish. We can heal ourselves internally and a miraculous life unfolds at our feet. We need our Divine Mother to kiss our wounds and make things better. And so, along with my Divine Mother, I've come to realize that I need to mother myself.

Mothering my heart

In another session with my life coach, Guy asked me to visualize myself holding my heart in my arms like it was a most precious baby. He asked me to picture myself loving it and caring for it like it was the most cherished and precious thing. I did, as tears came streaming down my face, remembering holding my two precious angels, Everett and Georgia, the same way when they were born. In that moment, I honoured my heart, my precious, blessed, cherished and sacred heart. "If your heart wasn't safe, secure and adored by you," he asked, "how would that make it feel?"

I read so many books about pregnancy and child rearing and stumbled across countless examples that provided scientific evidence of how babies could tell, even in utero, if they were wanted or not, if they were loved, welcomed and appreciated and if their mother thought they were precious. In fact, babies whose parents told them they were precious were seen to grow and thrive more than those whose parents didn't give them that kind of care. *Wouldn't the same be true for my heart?* I thought. Ugh. And then Guy said the words that were hard for me to hear: "You've been neglecting your heart for years, Tanya." Ouch. The truth hurts sometimes. "It's time all that changed," he said. And that's where the start of my heart acknowledgement and healing began. It became a regular practice for me. Whenever I feel the need, I put my hand on my heart, breathe and think of my heart like that precious baby. I sit with it and let it know that I'm here to love it and take care of it. It might sound hokey, but there's powerful research by Dr. David Hawkins, in his book *Letting Go: The Pathway to Surrender* to support it. It works.

CHAPTER 4 Reflections:

1. How do you mother yourself?
2. Do you connect with our Divine Mother? If so, how?
3. Does God, in your view, have a gender? Say more.
4. How have you healed past wounds? After you healed them, what opened up in your world?
5. What things do you wish your mother would have said to you? What things do you wish your grandmother would have said to your mother? If you have children, what are some of the most important things you want them to hear from you?
6. When you did the guided meditation, who was sitting at the desk and what word or words did they point you to? How do you translate that as a message you need to hear in your life right now?

5
Assemble a Sisterhood

"When I look around at this world, we women need each other so badly, it breaks my heart. Sisterhood is dissipating, and we aren't doing nearly enough to salvage it. Eliminate the crazies in your life, yes. But also look again at those around you."

~ GRACE GEALEY

Could everyone just take a moment to throw your hands in the air, and wave 'em like you just don't care (except you do) for the love and for the respect of your divine sisters and girlfriends! Cue the song "Friends" by Meghan Trainor and cheers to all of our sass-tacular vaginas! I don't know where I'd be without mine. My friends—not my vagina—although I don't know where I'd be without her either!

Assembling a sisterhood is vital to our ability to thrive in this world, yet the roles our sisters play don't always get the high-fives, kudos or props they deserve. *These* are the women who have helped us become the people we are today; they've shaped the narrative of our lives, actually. That goes for our friends today and even those no longer in the picture or not as much. As the Hebrew scripture says: "Iron shapes iron and friend shapes friend."

I'm so grateful for my sisters. I don't have any biological sisters, but I do have sisters-in-law whom I adore. Some of these relationships didn't come easy at first. Some didn't feel natural or effortless. But over time, we've grown into our own cohesive tribe. I love these women. Drop the "in-laws" part. They *are* my sisters. I'm so grateful for all we share together: the family members, the memories, the laughter and the commitment to being there for each other.

I love the friends in my life whom I consider my soul sisters too. These are women I deeply respect, admire and cherish. They are like diamonds, reflecting many different facets and sides, parts that are gentle, wise, loving, compassionate and kind, and other parts that are feisty warriors, sassy bitches and fierce lovers of humanity. Put 'em all together and they're stunning jewels, full of fire. They enrich my days by the virtue of them just breathing and being a part of my life. Female friendships or *femships* (move over bromances, there's a new duo in town!) are so important. The good ones will be this marvellous mix of women who make you laugh until you snort and a little pee runs down your thigh. They'll raise you up, encourage you when you feel like giving up and they'll always be kind to you—even when you're not being kind to yourself.

They talk you up and make you realize how damn amazing you are and give you that gentle nudge to get out there and show 'em what you're made of. They're loving and supportive and they just *get* you! They remind you of who you are especially in times when you've forgotten. They're with you throughout life's major milestones and through the mundane valleys too. They give you a reality check when you need it. They're cheerleaders along this road of life. When you fall, they're there to put their hands on your cheeks and smile, take your hand in theirs and pull you up. You'd do all this for them too. I could go on about the benefits of femships—they're a stress release, confidence booster, opportunity to learn new things and perspectives; they help you practice and experience love and loyalty. I think you understand. And I hope you've experienced—or are about to experience—all these things and more. In fact, I'd love for you to share your femship stories with me at tanyasood.com. I'm surprised there isn't more research out there about the value of friendships. But I know in my heart that they're one of the most precious things we can experience on earth and assembling a sisterhood can make life so much more enriching.

Shining together

There's nothing new about sisterhood. It's been the essential force behind the existence of tribes and ancient civilizations, but its importance often fades into society's background as does the notion that women are stronger together. It's my belief that the right femships can help us fulfill our potential and destiny while helping others do the same. That's pretty powerful stuff! So why don't we see more examples of femship in the media? Instead, we often see movie, television and even real-life sagas of women in conflict or competition with each other—and often over a man. What about their own experiences or goals? Or there's the cattiness satirized in the *Mean Girls*-esque movies. And these storylines start at an early age. Just look at *Snow White*, *Cinderella*, *Rapunzel* and relationships in *The Princess and the Pea*—intergenerational jealousy galore, competition and perpetual examples of women in conflict. Thank goodness we're seeing revamped fairytales today like Disney's *Frozen*,[29] *Pocahontas*,[30] *Brave*[31] and *Moana*,[32] where women are working together, being empowered and not needing to be rescued by a man. Instead, they're rescuing *themselves*. These examples are still few and far between. Where will the future inspiration come from for my young daughter? Could it come from you?

A tale of three sisters

It breaks my heart when I see women unnecessarily tearing down other women. I mean, it's bad enough when you see anyone tearing down another human being but especially actual sister to sister. I find it just painful to watch. There's a set of three sisters in my life, very close in age, and I've witnessed times when they've been so unkind to and unsupportive of each other. Once when one was in her late teens, she posted something on Facebook that was beyond honest, so courageously vulnerable that it brought proud tears to my eyes. It was a longer post where she bore her soul, talking about how nervous, worried and anxious she was feeling about going off to university. She had heard about all the essays and analyzing texts and selecting courses, and it all seemed so overwhelming to her. Pretty brave for a late teen in a public forum, huh? It brought me back to all the thoughts that were swirling through my head at that time in my life: *What am I going to do after high school? Will I continue with my studies and if so, what will my major be? What will my minor be? Why does selecting a minor feel so major? Will I do a victory lap and improve my grades? Will I take a year off and backpack through Europe? If so, will I do it alone or who might come with me? How am I going to pay for things? Student loans? Will I get a job at the end of this?* There was a lot going on upstairs at a time when I was just trying to get things off the ground and desperately needed support!

But back to the sisters. After the Facebook post, the slightly older sister, who was already in university, brought it up at a social gathering. I watched her try to publicly shame her younger sister with harsh words and a cruel tongue, telling her she better get used to it, the road ahead is hard, maybe she didn't have what it would take and even if she thought she did, she'd need to suck it up and deal. Mortified, I rose to the younger's defense but, sigh... like, really? Why do we do this to our sisters? I have one brother, six years my junior, so maybe I don't really know what it's like to grow up with a sister, but still, is this what it has really come to?

Why can't we support one another, especially in a moment of courageous vulnerability? Why can't we be kind to each other and support each other in our goals? And if it's not enough to do that from the goodness of our hearts without expectations for anything in return, I wanted to remind that sister that karma's a bitch.

Everything you're putting out there with your words and actions, especially when they're written or public, are all coming back to you. In fact, they have already been done to you. And for young people especially, who are trying to make their debut into the world, we need to encourage them to fly and inspire others to do the same so we can reach new heights together. When you're slinging mud at others, you're bound to get some splattered on yourself. And the biggest lie on the face of the planet is that saying, "Sticks and stones will break my bones but names will never hurt me." Nothing could be further from the truth, in my opinion. We must be as kind to our sisters as we are to ourselves.

A lot of this lack of support could stem from projection. It was a reminder to me that if I'm having a visceral reaction to someone for circumstances that hardly seem in proportion to my outburst, I need to pause and reflect. I've been there too. It's one of those moments of truth when I need to stop and ask myself, *What's hooking me?* or *What is it about that person that I can't stand about myself?* Over the years, I've learned that as amazing as girlfriends are, they can't fix everything. At the root, it's sometimes something I need to fix myself. To give myself. For me it means getting quiet, closing my eyes, putting my hand on my heart and listening to what my heart or soul or the little girl in me—or whatever body part is holding the hurt—needs. And saying to it, *It's okay. I got you. This is okay. We're going to be all right.* And breathing. Breathing a little more and staying with it. Over time it starts to dissipate. A chunk falls off. Maybe the next time it's a boulder. And being present with it as I later talk it over with a supportive girlfriend helps too.

It's important to recognize when this happens and kindly and gently support our sisters in need. I came to the defense of the sister going into university in a way that didn't make the older sister even more fired up but in a way that gently reminded her that we're all in this together, and we need to support each other through it. Because we're all sisters. We're all part of the same tribe. We need to be here for each other and preserve that sacredness that we experience in relationships with each other. All people need to have connections with women—it's something that traces back to the mother connection. This need is often fulfilled for men in relationships with women, but for women or gay men, girlfriends can satiate this need. We need to work with each other and hold each other up instead of tearing each other apart. It also comes back to that Golden Rule—what I glean from the bible the most—and that's to treat others—in this case, your friends—as you would like to be treated. Reciprocity. Empathy. Observe these and your friendships will remain strong and hearty despite pests, drought, wind and weather.

Rachel Sklar is a New York City writer, social entrepreneur and co-founder of TheLi.st, a network and platform for professional women who are ambitious, accomplished and committed to helping each other rise. Rachel says the lack of focus on the power of female friendship is a result of the way our culture erases female power and the bonds that women make. That's why she created TheLi.st with co-founder Glynnis MacNicol. It's a refreshing example of a community of women that is interested and supportive of each other's professional success.

Strong friendships with powerful women have many benefits, including helping women get ahead. It's the basis of the "shine theory," a term coined by Ann Friedman in *New York Magazine*. Shine theory refers to the way that being around fabulous women can make you more likely to be fabulous yourself. These women shine light; they don't cast shadows. Cases in point—famous female pairings such as Amy Poehler and Tina Fey, or Shonda Rhimes and Betsy Beers. They serve as examples of how long-standing female friendships help women advance professionally. Rebel Wilson, an actress who has the power to make me explode with hysterical laughter, says that like many of us, she has a special place in her heart for the 1992 movie *A League of Their Own*[33] directed by Penny Marshall. Rebel says that cast had special meaning for her. "It's about women joining together and being empowered but also about sisters sticking together even when there's drama and struggles."

No patience anymore for the cocktail conversations of life

I'm so over cocktail conversations. I'm so *tired* of small talk. I want rich, robust and meaningful conversations that make me feel like we're in this together and helping each other figure it all out as we go. Meaningful connections need to be grounded in realness and vulnerability. You know what I mean? Like if I'm going to show up at your house for a girls' night in an oversized powder blue bathrobe that I bought when I was pregnant (eight years ago) with chip and cheese crumbs down the front and three litres of pinot grigio in a box, I need for you not to judge me. Because we are going to talk about some truly amazing and enriching things, and we all need to be comfortable and able to be ourselves with the people close to us without the fear of being judged or ostracized or any feelings of competition or one-up-man-*or woman*-ship. We need to be real and show up, just as we are.

We are enough—standing still with our socks on.

A couple years ago I took weekly yoga classes with my dear friend, Amy, who introduced me to Gayla, her friend and the yoga instructor. These women became like beacons of light for me at a time when I was going through shifting times with one of my closest friends. Their kindness, realness, support and care for me starkly contrasted that very close friendship in my life. I found it hard to face the truth that it had been dying a slow death for a number of years. It no longer felt good to be around her; I felt like she was incapable of being happy for me, she judged me – her body language alone spoke volumes. She took up all the space and the airtime and she just didn't seem interested in my life. In fact, she seemed bored the moment I opened my mouth or shared something about me. It left me feeling bad about myself, angry or depleted of energy. I knew I needed to make a change, I just didn't know how to go about it. But I was starting to get a sense that just because it was comfortable, didn't mean it was good for me.

Amy and Gayla uplifted me. They fully accepted me. They listened to what was on my mind and they comforted, inspired and saw the best in me. We even started doing this ritual together and with a group of other like-minded women where we'd sit on lawn chairs in Gayla's backyard and have a campfire on the night of the full moon each month. We'd write down three things that were no longer serving us. Sometimes that list included people. After we shared them with the group and listened supportively and helped each other through what we were experiencing, we'd burn those little pieces of paper! Set them ablaze in the campfire! It was awesome – I love burning things! And then we wrote down a list of three new things we wanted to usher into our lives to serve us and so we could better serve others. We lit those on fire too – because burning things is fun! (within reason). This was such a supportive group for me. Not only did I feel accepted, I felt a sense of belonging with a group of people I could relate to. I even shared the beginnings of this book with them and they were all like, "Right on! Cheers to your vagina! I can't wait to read your book. Keep going, Tanya – you're brilliant and we love you!" Like seriously! I had no idea people like this even existed, but they do! And I swear I attracted them too because when I was going through the stuff with my other friend, I'd dream of a different kind of friendship. One that was supportive, spiritual, caring and funny! I envisioned us talking about new age-y stuff without feeling like we were alone, out on a limb or judged. I'd watch movies like *It's Complicated*[34] and see how Meryl Streep, Rita Wilson, Mary Kay Place and Alexandra Wentworth would support and love up on each other – laughing about vaginoplasties and girly chatter. I love that movie! I love that example of female friendships and I've watched that movie so many times, it drives my husband crazy! But, the result: I found my own version – they just came to me one day as a gift that fell from the Universe. It set a new standard and my friendships have never been the same.

Being what you want to be in this world means putting that energy out there and attracting it back to yourself. That takes presence, consciousness and courage. As one of my favourite authors and speakers, Brené Brown explains: "Courage is a heart word. The root of the word courage is cor - the Latin word for heart. In one of its earliest forms, the word courage meant "To speak one's mind by telling all one's heart." Over time, this definition has changed, and today, we typically associate courage with heroic and brave deeds. But in my opinion, this definition fails to recognize the inner strength and level of commitment required for us to actually speak honestly and openly about who we are and about our experiences — good and bad. Pushing past surface conversations and instead speaking from our hearts takes ordinary courage but yields deep, meaningful returns.

When your evolution shines a light on a friendship

Harvard University researcher, Nicholas Christakis, found that social networks have a viral and "contagious" nature; that is, we take on the habits of those people who surround us. So apply the right filters. My father used to always tell me to be mindful of who I hung out with and it turns out, he was right! The people we surround ourselves with will have more of an effect on what we do and who we become than many other factors.

That's why there are times when we need to step back and take stock of the strongest influences in our lives. Are they the right ones? Are they healthy, uplifting and helping us serve the world as our best selves? I like to spend more of my time with people who stretch me a little to think outside of my traditional way of thinking. Outside of the box. Outside of *my* box. Boxes aside, there's this great analogy that Bishop T.D. Jakes gives about giraffes and turtles. He mentions it in his book *Instinct: The Power to Unleash Your Inborn Drive*, and he also addresses the concept in an *Oprah Life Class* interview. Jakes says the giraffe and the turtle may occupy the same space, but they don't have the same worldview. Now, if you haven't seen the video clip of this, I highly recommend you

Google it and watch it for the audience's reaction alone! It's priceless. They're so animated. I love it. But it really speaks to how things evolve and how people evolve. There might have been a time when you were a turtle (I was), and things made sense to you and your turtle friends. But as we choose to evolve, we get a broader worldview and that can escalate to the scale of what's witnessed by a giraffe. It becomes the giraffe's reality. But when we remain friends with the turtles, they can criticize what we see in contrast to what they see, and this may come across as unsupportive. Because they're playing to what you were as a turtle, and not letting you evolve to what you've become as a giraffe.

And, as T.D. Jakes points out, the giraffe has a 25-pound heart so that it will pump blood up its 9-foot neck, so that its head can stay high. Conversely, he says, if the giraffe lowers its head to the level of the turtle, he will lose consciousness and pass out. "And when you were built to be tall, you will endanger your position if you lower your perspective," he says. "And there's nothing wrong with the turtle, because the turtle would give you an honest report from their perspective. But you cannot explain to a turtle a giraffe decision!"[35]

So what do you do with your turtle relationships?

Years ago, I remember reading a quote about keeping company only with those who uplift you. At the time, I subscribed to the theory. I could get pretty all-or-nothing with things back then—it's what I had been taught. Growing up, I had watched my parents weed out people from their lives who they believed were no longer serving them. They did it in an honest effort to preserve themselves and our family. But over the years, I've learned that a shift can happen when you've outgrown a friendship, and it doesn't have to be an all-or-nothing thing. You don't have to break up with your girlfriends unless, of course, someone's crossed the line and violated something major that would result in a deal breaker. I'm not suggesting enduring unkindness or cruelty for the sake of holding on. Put those toxic relationships aside, but there are some friendships that can be salvaged and transformed into something different.

I'm talking about a shift from receiving to giving. When considering if you've outgrown a friendship, ask yourself if it's time for you to give back—for you as a giraffe to be there from time to time for the betterment of the turtle.

It can be a fine balance, I know. You must manage feeling depleted or resentful in the revamped friendship. Set some parameters around it in your head. For example, you could say to yourself: *I'm going to go out for coffee with this person four times a year and I'm going to schedule something after to time-box* (ha! Another box!) *it so I don't feel like I'm giving more than I have*. You could promise yourself that during that hour, or hour and a half, you're going to be fully present, listen and try to help and support that person because you believe in goodness and feel it's the right thing to do. And you can look for things in that person that you might not have noticed before, and try to see her good. After all, she's got divinity inside her too.

It also helps not to put all your eggs in one friendship basket. That's what I did with the friend I was describing earlier. She was my go-to person. I didn't really branch out much and invest in other friendships. That's part of what kept me holding on for so long while my resentment grew. After I figured out the shift, things changed for the better. I could be there for her at a time and in a way that she needed me to be. And that felt right for me.

Assembling your sisterhood can be a sobering exercise that forces you to evaluate who is really contributing to your life. Who are your supporters? Are you spending the right amount of time with them? Who would have your back? Who do you want to give back to? Who values what you say and do and who you are without judgment, ridicule or lack of interest. Is the relationship a two-way street? Because it's a relationship—it needs to be.

You've heard about how women who live together eventually synchronize their periods to flow at the same time, right? It's because the people you surround yourself with become an extension of your energy, which is why it's so important to ensure your team members are uplifting each other, and are aligned with you and that they're as much a cheerleader to you as you are to them. They help us show up in this world as our best selves so that we can give back to others with positive energy and light.

Female bonding is as old as the hills

Women used to live and work together in tribes and villages. When a woman was pregnant, other women of the tribe would help her through it, help her rest and bring her the comfort of what she needed. After she gave birth, the child would be taken care of by a series of "aunties" within the tribe. This is where that "it takes a village" saying originated. They'd give the mother the time and space she needed to rest and recover from the miracle her body just performed. They'd cook for her and bring her teas and herbal remedies to help her on her way. This is still practiced in many traditions but often feels worlds apart from the experience of many women—in North America anyway.

No, here we're raced along to the hospital to have a baby, be in-and-out of there in a matter of hours or short days and we get on with it. I had an emergency C-section with my daughter, and I was in isolation because I also had the flu, and I was in-and-out of the hospital within two days. It was major abdominal surgery. Immediate family members had to wear gowns and gloves to come in the room. Like seriously, what has this world come to? Why aren't we working together more as women to support each other through such events? I hope the world is changing.

I remember attending a Belly Blessing Ceremony for one of my friends while she was pregnant. Instead of the typical baby shower with silly games and colourful sandwiches, it had a much more serious and sacred tone. Only the people who she felt would honour the ritual were invited, and we started by saying a few prayers for my friend, along with reading a series of poems. We also read our wishes for her. We made a bracelet for her with a bead we had each brought, and we asked for it to be blessed for her. We even washed her feet in a basin with warm water, essential oils and flower petals and we massaged her feet, hands and shoulders to show her our love and support. And when she was in labour, we received word and each of the girls present lit a candle we were given at the ceremony and offered our prayer.

Why don't we do more of this stuff? And in this man's world, why do we so often feel we need to be tough or something and work right up until our due date and act like the watermelon growing inside us is really no biggie. Sometimes a period alone is a biggie! Our bodies are miracle factories, people—we're making life here! Why don't we give ourselves and our bodies the credit they deserve? Let's love up on each other, love our sisters. Help hold each other up. We have been oppressed. Let's not turn against each other just when we're catching our stride and need each other's support the most.

CHAPTER 5 Reflections:

1. Who makes up your sisterhood?
2. What qualities do the sisters in your sisterhood share?
3. What are your thoughts regarding Shine Theory? What are some other examples of Shine Theory that you've witnessed? Who helps you shine and who do you help shine?
4. How do you cultivate a deeper sense of sisterhood with the women in your life?
5. What have these women done for you? What have you done for them?
6. Describe a relationship that moved from the turtle to the giraffe analogy. What happened? Why do you think it happened? What have you learned?
7. What are three things that are no longer serving you? I'm saying *things* here, but it could include a person or people too. Write them down. What are three things you want to usher into your life now? Write them down too. Gather up a circle of close girlfriends, have a campfire and burn those pieces of paper. Let 'em burn baby! It's a ritual. Do it on the night of the full moon and it's even more powerful! It has meaning and it feels amazing!

6
Overcome Fear

"You gain strength, courage, and confidence by every experience in which you really stop to look fear in the face. You must do the thing which you think you cannot do."

~ELEANOR ROOSEVELT

Fear is what separates the imprisoned from the free. I spent far too many years in a perpetual state of fear. It was exhausting. And it's no surprise really. Fear is physically and emotionally draining! Physically, it feels like an anchor chained to your hip and stuck to the bottom of the sea. Debilitating doesn't adequately describe it. Let's just say it's impossible to stay there for too long because it robs you of your oxygen. And emotionally? It's like you don't even have the energy to experience an emotion because fear's already kicked your emotions' ass and drained their life force.

Once I was fruitfully employed at a financial services company. The pay and benefits were great, the senior leadership was inspiring and the office building had a cafeteria, gym and even a prayer room (in case interest rates dipped really low!). Everything looked great on paper except I was giving all my power to my boss and it was costing me my soul. She was a full-time job to manage – perpetually underwhelmed no matter how hard I tried. I was so busy trying to duck out of the way of her narcissism, confusing comments, looks and controlling demands that I wore myself out and allowed fear (chased by exhaustion) to take over. *Would she fire me if I made a mistake? Would she allow me to have a difference of opinion? Would she give me a good reference or would she throw me under the bus?* Looking back, I shudder.

What I didn't know then but I do know now is that I wasn't living in alignment with my values. The exterior didn't match my interior, and that compromised my integrity, even if it was just me who noticed. On the exterior it looked like I had it all together. I wore the navy suits, chunky jewellery and my hair hung impeccably straight. I walked fast and my gestures were slow and controlled. I could whip together strategy documents, Venn diagrams (oh, the vesica pisces!), executive communications, change management plans and marketing presentations like nobody's business. I was told I was poised, confident and calm in a crisis (although the rash on my face was starting to give me away). I think my voice even dropped an octave while I was working there (so much male energy). But on the interior, my soul was screaming at me—and six octaves higher. Instead of expressing emotions with her along the way, I was holding stuff in for fear of rocking the boat. The irony was IT WAS A COMMUNICATIONS ROLE! And I wasn't effectively communicating. And it was a performance culture and I was trying to please the unpleasable. By the time I left that role, I despised her and I wanted to be free. But looking back, it was really me who imprisoned myself. I had the key and the door unlocked from the inside.

I had a voice. I always have a voice. I'm not a victim and I have choices. It wasn't until I started writing this book that I realized what it felt like to be energized and back in alignment with my values. Why? Because I was using my voice through my writing. For years, I had been writing speeches, presentations, articles, research papers, media releases, communications and strategic plans for *other people*. For senior executives. It was my job to make them look good and I was good at my job! During my last few months in that role alone, I wrote speeches that received standing ovations from crowds. One had a room of more than 1,500 people on their feet for the words *I* put in that executive's mouth! And those leaders valued me and recognized me often with positive feedback; they had come to rely on me to help them to shine. So then why was I so afraid to go out on a limb and say my *own* words? To do my own thing? To speak my truth? To let my soul fly? It started to amaze me—like I got really curious about how fear had this kind of powerful hold over me. And then I started to ask myself, *Where would I be right now if I didn't have this fear?* When I allowed that question to run through the halls of my heart, things started shifting. I started to see my fear for what it was: an illusion.

There are all sorts of fears. They come in many varieties: fear of authority; fear of not knowing enough; fear of failure; fear of not making enough money; fear of making too much money; fear of judgment; fear of loss of control; fear of being rejected; fear of dying or being physically harmed and the big whoppers: fear of not being loved or enough.

As soon as we understand what kind of fear is holding us back, we can address it. Sometimes that's all it takes—looking that fear straight in the eye and simply starting to notice it.

The book *Taming Your Gremlin* by Rick Carson was a life-changing read for me. Rick paraphrased the *Zen Theory of Change* by boiling it down to this, "I free myself not by trying to be free, but by simply noticing how I am imprisoning myself in the very moment I am imprisoning myself."[36] A bit of a head scratcher, but it goes back to that mindfulness exercise of simply noticing. It also reminds me of what Andy Putticombe says in headspace.com about picturing your mind as a blue sky. Thought clouds will come and go, and you can simply notice them instead of trying to run after them, grab hold of them, analyze or judge them. The act of simply noticing is the first step in overcoming fear. It brings you to the here and now. It centres you and removes the power of those fears and cruel and doubting voices.

I love how Carson describes his whole theory about Gremlins too. It's about noticing the voices in your head. Write the words down if that's easier for you, and just look at them. Simply notice what's there. *Wow, there's a thought. There's my Gremlin; here's what he or she is saying. Humpf. There he goes again.* Simply noticing is such a different position than I've taken in the past! Before, I'd try to squeeze that little bastard in my firmest grip possible and analyze the hell out of him. *Where is this coming from? How did that thought get there?* I'd want to expose it to sunlight, keep it dry to avoid it multiplying and not feed the little bastard until after midnight so I could get 'em the hell out of my life. Turns out, it doesn't work that way. Because you and I both know, we could analyze until we're blue in the face, until the cows come home and the milk (or wine) runs dry. Doesn't matter. We could keep going like an Energizer Bunny about it. Instead, we begin to deflate the little buggers by simply noticing them. It's like the spotlight melts them and shrivels them into these little babies and we can feel quite sorry for them. *Poor little things.* And that can allow us to work with them through the lens of compassion rather than against them.

I've talked with a lot of women over the years, and it seems like their fears come through stronger than men. I don't know if this is scientifically proven; it's just my observation. I've often wondered if something on a cellular level has made fear more prominent for women at times or more difficult to move past. I can't help but wonder if some of it traces back to the Middle Ages when the church decided to give God a masculine image and stripped away or ostracized all that was female. They regarded the pentagram, the symbol of the Sacred Feminine in Pagan culture, as evil and the symbol for Satan. And that led to the whole *Malleus Malifcarum* or *Hammer of the Witches*, which was a book released *by the church*, and regarded as the bloodiest book in history. The book regarded all women who read or researched as witches and described ways to torture and kill them.

And even before that—and tracing back to the birth of Jesus over 2,000 years ago—the Christian church has supported and participated in the oppression of women. It has been an oppression that has been both covert and overt; unconscious and conscious. It has come primarily through the church's ability, in the name of God, to define a woman and to make that definition stick. It was grounded in a literal interpretation of Holy Scripture, thought of as the infallible word of God and produced in a patriarchal era.[37] Patriarchy and God have been so deeply and uncritically linked to gender by the all-male church hierarchy that men have little understanding of how this alliance has been used to the detriment of women.[38] How has this impacted our fear, and where are our spiritual role models to offer us rays of hope?

Well, if we look further back in history, they can be found. Goddesses such as Inanna or Ishtar, Isis, Venus, the Green Tara, the Black Madonna, Lala, Tara Ma and Kali. Look mamas, in prehistoric and early historic periods of human development, there were religions that revered their supreme creator as female. Based on archaeological evidence, scholars believe that the Great Goddess, the Divine Ancestress, was worshiped as far back as the Upper Paleolithic about 25,000 BC–7000 BC, and the last Goddess temples were closed about 500 AD.[39]

Remembering these Divine Feminine figures and what they've been through can help us face our fears. All that is lurking ominously—either deeply buried in our inner darkness or closer to the surface—needs to be stared in the eye and brought into the light of consciousness. Are our fears serving us by warning us about dangerous places, things, or people? Or are our fears preventing us from dancing our own unique dance, living our lives, creating with Creation?

It's human nature to resist change and fear the unknown. But these Divine Feminine figures teach us that accepting change, fear and the unknown while grieving for what we've lost in the past and the pain and sadness of letting go is sometimes necessary to continue on our path to having a fulfilling life. Wholeness is nurtured when we reclaim the pieces of ourselves that we've given over to fear. Most fears are formless, and Rick Carson would have us believe these fears or Gremlins are almost cartoon-like. By naming and witnessing the fear or Gremlin, we gain power. Wholeness is created when we learn to acknowledge our fears and overcome them.

Looking for Mother comfort in the face of fear

As the patriarchal religions slowly began to replace earlier matriarchal ones, we lost touch with the Divine Mother and the feminine qualities she possesses. And we re-created our culture with only a father, valuing only to the elements traditionally or symbolically associated with fathers, maleness and masculinity. It's a tragic spiritual situation that could be likened to a baby being born into the world and then being denied the loving attention associated with mothering. This is true for both women and men!

Reverend Ricky Hoyt, a Unitarian Universalist minister, author and spiritual director serving two congregations in the Los Angeles area, described this in detail in a sermon. He invited people to imagine a baby born unexpectedly and violently out of the womb.[40] The only universe it has known, dark and wet, muted and warm, is suddenly replaced by a brightly lit, noisy, unbounded space filled with air, not water.[41] The child's first reaction is certainly terror and an overwhelming sense of abandonment and loneliness.[42] Some methods of birthing attempt to mitigate these responses, but like Rev. Ricky Hoydt, I'm not convinced that they can be removed entirely. The birthing process itself describes a sudden and complete world change for the child.[43] It's the mother who eases that transition. She holds the child against beating heart, a familiar sound, to bring the baby comfort and a feeling of safety. The child isn't alone. He or she is held and loved. The child isn't abandoned. Mother is there.

But what if Mother isn't there? Spiritually, this is the situation for so many of us within our cultures and religions. We know the trauma this causes real children—the wounded psyches and shattered lives that follow.[44] Born without a spiritual mother, our initial experience of spiritual terror is confirmed, not eased. Reverend Hoyt says, "the world can be a scary place, our patriarchal religions and governments confirm our sense of terror, encourage our terror, and are not above using our terror and even manufacturing new terrors in order to keep us fearful and thus dependent on the strong father whose symbolic mode is not comfort but protection, not healing, but war-making.[45]" For traditional patriarchal religions, he says, God is distant, majestic, transcendent and an "other, unapproachable, vastly different from and far beyond us" God. He loves us and showers us with gifts but not with himself. The gifts stand between him and us. While the Divine Mother, the one whose womb has been symbolically denied to us, gives directly of herself. There is no separation. Indeed, in the womb we don't even feel that it is us and her; it is just us—a singular, satisfying sense of being.[46]

That's what we lost when we lost our spiritual mothers. And we're a long way from home. I mean no disrespect to the male or masculine side of God. They are good and important. And as Reverend Hoyd points out, "many of the negatives associated with masculinity are not actually inherent in masculinity but are aberrations based on a sick and broken culture which has short-changed men from their own health and wholeness by labelling some of his true self feminine and therefore to be suppressed, unnaturally, from his personality."[47] But God isn't a Divine Father who lives in the sky. God is beyond sex and gender. God is Being. God is God. And that is something that has been lost in a series of translations over thousands of years.

So where do we go from here? I'm not suggesting that we transform the Divine Father into the Divine Mother or marry them off. I'm suggesting we revert to the essence of the Divine that hasn't changed over time as we've imposed our values on it. The Divine is already complete and speaks to us as both mother and father. It is our ears that need to open. It's our spiritual practice and spiritual imaginations that need to change and receive what has been there all along. We must let go of what is no longer serving us.

Honouring body and soul

As I mentioned earlier, sometimes we need to remove the boulders piling up in our hearts that can get stuck in the way. Have you experienced this? It's been a hard lesson for me. I used to tend to get far too stuck in my head. I'd think my way through life—still do at times and need to bring myself back—and then when I was done thinking about things, I'd think some more, sometimes about what I just thought about or what I needed to think about more (or less). It was insidious. And then I'd often be hard on myself and give myself a hard time for thinking so much or thinking and judging, and it turns into this vicious, ugly cycle.

When I was working for that old boss where I wasn't honouring my soul, I spent a lot of time living in my thoughts. Thinking my way through what I thought was rational. I had a good job with good pay; I was providing for my family. I was using my head about things until I found that it was coming at a cost of my heart, my soul and my own voice.

I talked this out with my coach. A lot of my sentences started with, "I think that..." and "I think it's because..." He asked me to tell him not what I was thinking but what I was feeling. And where I was experiencing that feeling in my body? I felt these things below my neck. As I talked more about this misalignment and dug into it while trying to pay attention to where it was showing up in my body, I realized I was giving all this attention to the thoughts in my head at the expense of ignoring my heart—and my body as a whole—and that was making my soul really angry.

When I took the time to tap into that anger, I learned that my anger was a secondary emotion to the primary one, which was fear. It surfaced only in pockets of my body that I had been ignoring. There was a fiery blaze that went from the pit of my stomach to the lump in my throat. Guy asked me how my heart felt trapped in between. It felt numb. "So you have this fiery blaze in your gut and a lump in throat, but you don't really feel anything in your heart, which is found between?" Guy asked me. And that's when the record scratched. That's when I really noticed that I had been living most of my life in head, so much so that my body was getting angry and my heart was feeling completely ignored. Living mostly in my head, my friends, is a dangerous place to be! It can be like this dusty old attic full of memories, judgments, fears and disappointments. Not a place I want to live. I want to live in the kitchen, the *heart* of the home, where things are vibrant and fresh and nourishing.

If I was really honest with myself, it's then that I realized I was rarely living in my body. For the longest time, before I realized the significance of the body, the vesica piscis and our divinity inside it, it's like my body was a place I didn't want to go to or spend time in. I had spent so much time terrorizing my body with thoughts and comparisons and berating and belittling it. It had been background noise in my life and I took over the dialogue internally. I had been blocking the passage into my body with rejection instead of ushering myself in with acceptance to live and dwell and love and feel joy within it. I thought my body didn't matter for the longest time. I judged others who were so focused on their bodies. I thought they were egotistical and vain and superficial. I was more into the mind and put value in that, but I realized that it was at the expense of my body. One doesn't need to come at the expense of the other! And what I didn't acknowledge at the time was that our bodies are temples. It's true. They house our souls. It's like the church of your spirit. And I had been ignoring, poo-pooing it for years. That was a mistake. And I needed to let go to release the fear that was blocking me from honouring my heart and soul.

Now letting go and acceptance are very closely connected (as is faith but more on that in Chapter 8), and because I had be struggling with it for so long and didn't know how to release my fear, I turned to our Divine Mother for help, love, support and guidance. In meditation, again I envisioned sitting on her lap, leaning my head on her chest and feeling her heart bursting open with love—unconditional divine love—and a sense of knowing that she saw me as perfect just the way I was. There was nothing I needed to do or change; she deeply loved me for being me. I felt this nurturing love and I felt so held and secure by her and seen. She saw and loved everything about me. I envisioned my heart being wide open and our Divine Mother giving me a bath in her glorious rays of light. It was golden light that cleared away negativity and any of my problems and worries that were dragging me down. This bright golden white light was moving through me, clearing and cleaning away anything ready to be released. I sat quietly feeling the light rays moving through me, and then I opened up to her with my concerns or problems. She listened to me and I envisioned her telling me to listen to my intuition and that she would be there helping to guide me. "I am always with you," she assures me. "I am always here to love, support, honour and guide you."

I encourage you to sit in quiet meditation or reflection and connect with our Divine Mother too. Especially when it comes to your fears. She is pure energy. Glorious light. The most magnificent mother you could even imagine and more. Claire Huxtable, Elyse Keaton and Carol Brady ain't got nothin' on our Divine Mother. It's like all of them times infinity! She has the answers. She has so much love to give us. She is always there and wants to form a relationship with us. That is God. That is the Divine Feminine side of God—always there for you. And what was the fear I brought to her that day? It was my fear of moving from a job that didn't honour my soul to a writing and speaking career that did and my fear of failing at it or not being ready to write this book. Her response, which was echoed by my life coach later that day was, "What if you're ready enough?"

Coincidence? I don't think so. Living in fear is like living in the shadows and it's an illusion anyway. As Mike Dooley said in one of his *"Notes from the Universe:"*

> "If you could see the whole, you'd discover that the unpleasantness was only the tiniest piece of a most spectacular puzzle that was created with order,

intelligence, and absolute love. You'd see that contrary to appearances, in the grandest scheme of things, nothing is ever lost, no one becomes less, and setbacks are always temporary. And you'd understand that no matter what has happened, everyone lives again, everyone laughs again, and everyone loves again, even more richly than before."[48]

Booyah.

CHAPTER 6 Reflections:

1. What fears are holding you back?
2. If you could draw your fears as comical cartoons, what would they look like? What would you name them?
3. How could you acknowledge a fear and shine a light on it without giving it power? What would you say to it?
4. What would life be like without those fears?
5. What fears have you overcome to get you to where you are and how did you do it?
6. How do you honour what you're feeling not only in your head but in your body too?
7. What do you think the opposite of fear is?

7
Take Action and Receive Divine Gifts

"When I was in the middle of writing Eat Pray Love and I fell into one of those pits of despair that we will fall into when we're working on something that's not coming and we think 'this is going to be a disaster, this is going to be the worst book I've ever written — not just that but the worst book ever written... So I just lifted my face up from the manuscript and I directed my comments to an empty corner of the room and I said aloud 'Listen you, thing! You and I both know that if this book isn't brilliant that is not entirely my fault, right? Because you can see I am putting everything I have into this, I don't have any more than this, so if you want it to be better then you've got to show up and do your part of the deal, OK? But you know what? If you don't do that then I'm going to keep writing because that's my job and I would please like the record to reflect today that I showed up and did my part of the job!"

~ ELIZABETH GILBERT

In March 2015, I attended a writer's workshop weekend in Chicago hosted by Hay House Publishing. I was travelling on my own and decided to make the most of my time by flying from a small local airport near my house instead of driving to the larger international one an hour away. At the time, my idea for the book was still coming together, and I thought it would be a great opportunity for me to learn about how to write a book proposal. So off I went to experience what turned out to be an unforgettable weekend. I heard from guest speakers including Mike Dooley, the author, speaker and inventor of the sensational online phenomenon *"Notes from the Universe."* We also heard from Reid Tracey, Hay House CEO, and Nancy Levin who had just turned author after playing a behind-the-scenes role at Hay House for a number of years. I was inspired by their words of wisdom and couldn't wait to get home to write my book proposal. As an attendee, I had a chance to get a book deal with Hay House or money toward two self-publishing contracts. I was so excited! After the conference ended on Sunday night, I called my husband and kids from the airport. I had arrived early because I wanted to grab a bite to eat at the Chicago Cubs Bar and Grill. And I had to pick up a bag of Garrett popcorn, of course!

My call home was leisurely. I had time to give my husband an overview of how the conference ended that day, and I talked with my kids before it was time for them to have a bath and get ready for bed. I air kissed them through the phone and told them I'd come into their bedroom that night to give them a real kiss while they were sleeping. As I hung up, I noticed it was starting to snow, which seemed a little unusual for the end of March, but the snowflakes seemed fluffy and harmless. I wheeled my bag over to the gate.

When I approached the airport monitor, I did a double take. My flight had been *cancelled* to Waterloo? WTF? My flight couldn't be cancelled. I needed to get home! After a series of phone calls, tears and finally getting through to a real, live person, I came to grips with the reality that my flight had been cancelled because of weather. There was a storm coming into Chicago, and while my husband said it was sunny back home, the weather detectors at the airport near our house had shut down (we later learned). The airline was able to get me onto another flight the following day (thankfully I took Monday off work), as long as I got back to the airport at 3:00 a.m. for my 6:00 a.m. flight to...*Philadelphia?* Yes, it appeared I was going to be zig-zagging across the freakin' USA before catching a connecting flight north to Canada. And not even to the airport I flew out of but to Toronto, which was an hour away from my home. Fine. Toronto was the least of my worries. It was now 9:00 p.m. on Sunday. They sent me on my way to find a hotel to stay "overnight" (i.e. the next six hours).

So I called a hotel and made a reservation, then found my way through O'Hare—which isn't easy to do, I might add—to the pick-up area where a shuttle would take me to my hotel. Once I arrived at the hotel, they couldn't find my name among their reservations, and I was about to cry all over again at this point because there were so many hotels associated with that chain that I thought I might've gotten off at the wrong one. Finally, they settled things and I was shown to my room. I was completely frazzled and called my husband. I joked that there was a bar downstairs and if I wasn't a woman alone in a city where I didn't know anyone (more fear), I'd be tempted to go and have a drink. "Go have a drink!" he said. "You've earned it!" He had a point.

It was a nice bar, reminded me of *Cheers*. I sat up at the bar and the bartender even asked to see my ID. *Thank you, Universe!* As I sipped my pinot grigio (ice cold, just the way I like it), I thought about the day and all that had happened and the fact that I was grateful for that moment. I was safe,

I had a flight home, I had a glass of wine in my hand and I had even been mistaken for being younger than twenty-one! Life was good.

But by the time I returned to the airport early the next morning, that moment of gratitude was fading. It had started snowing quite heavily by the time we boarded the plane. The flight staff was de-icing the wings, and it took longer than they expected so we ended up being delayed by close to an hour. I was freaking out thinking I was going to miss my plane in Philadelphia because I only had an hour between the two flights. I was sitting beside a girl who introduced herself as Elya. Fast friends, Elya and I promptly decided to freak out together. She was supposed to be in Philadelphia so she could take another flight to meet her mother. She had auditions coming up for the lead role of Ariel in the musical, *The Little Mermaid,* and she needed to get there fast. And I, well I just needed to get home to my family. First-world problem, I know but an important one to me.

As we waited on the frozen tarmac, Elya started humming *"A Part of Your World"* from the musical. I felt strangely at peace and grateful for this stranger who was calming my nerves. She was so gentle and kind. She asked about my kids and shared that she had been a nanny for three children while she was in college. I could tell by the way her face lit up when she spoke of the children that she genuinely loved kids. I was grateful for her. She made a turbulent flight go smoothly for me.

When we finally landed, we were trying to organize ourselves into those who had connecting flights and those who didn't so those of us who did could burst ahead of the crowd like an old-school Kool-Aid commercial and try to catch the next plane. I sprinted across the Philadelphia airport like I was making my Olympic debut, and when I finally arrived at the gate—close to hyperventilating, my back soaking with sweat and my limbs feeling like they were going to break off from my body because I was running with all my stuff—the seating area was empty. There wasn't even an attendant at the gate. With a sinking feeling in my chest, I watched my plane taxi down the runway.

Panicking—for the, well, I had lost count how many times at this point—I called my husband. Then I called the airline, the other airlines, and the airport—I wanted to call the air*plane*. I called everyone I could think of who might be able to help me. And to make a long story short, the airline said the best they could do was get me on a plane on Wednesday morning. It was Monday at 11:00 a.m. And that, my friends, was *not* going to work. So I marched my feisty hot-and-bothered ass downstairs to the rental car phone booths, I called one of them up and got myself one of the last cars they had. I was going to *drive* home to Canada. Well, to Tonawanda, New York actually because the rental car company wouldn't allow me to take the car across the border. I got one of the last vehicles as a ton of other travellers had the same idea. O'Hare had shutdown at that point. I had no money, and the bank machine wouldn't take my debit card. Thankfully the taxi to the rental car company accepted credit cards. I arrived at the rental car pick-up point heaving, where they offered me a dinky little car that wasn't a standard and wasn't fully automatic but somewhere in between. I realized this about four hours into driving when I changed gears and it made the drive a whole lot smoother! Anyhoo, I was on my way to Tonawanda and thankfully, my husband arranged for a babysitter to take care of the kids so he could come pick me up at the border and take me home. Altogether, it would be about a ten-hour journey. Crikey.

Before leaving the rental company, I asked for a map. Smart idea, right? Because I had *no idea* where I was going! I had never been to Philadelphia before and I needed to find my way to Tonawanda? How the fuck was I going to do that? "I'm sorry, we don't have any maps," the rental car salesman said to me. Racing thoughts. Deep breath. *Okay. Let me just get this straight in my head first: so...you're a rental car company but you don't have any...FUCKING MAPS?!?!?* "But here's a bottle of water," he said. "In fact, why don't you take two; you have a long drive ahead of you." Yes, yes I did. I just prayed that the GPS on my phone would get me there. Oh, and I didn't have my power cord with me either. Sigh.

I had no idea where I was going. Even looking back, it was all a bit of a blur. I just remember there were turnpikes, twists, turns and tollbooths galore. I kept trying to see the wider view of the map on my phone but the application was stuck, allowing me only to see a short distance. I worried about ending up in New York City (which wouldn't be so bad except I was supposed to go to work in the morning). I worried about driving off the coast. I worried about the mountains I saw in the distance—would I have to drive through them? I was worried sick the entire trip. I didn't realize it at the time but my hands were gripping the steering wheel so tightly that the middle finger of my right hand was stiff and cramped for weeks after that trip! And navigating it all was crazy! At one point, I forgot to take a ticket at a tollbooth or I must've mistakenly driven through the EZ Pass lane, so when I came up to the next toll and they asked for my ticket I said I needed one because I didn't have one. "You don't have a ticket? I'm going to have to charge you forty-six dollars then." Jerk. I had sixty in cash on me and hours to go, so I was hoping on a prayer that either fourteen dollars would cover it or my debit card would start working again.

And so I drove. And I drove and I drove and I drove. And for a while, I relaxed a little when I found a good radio station with some empowering tunes. But truth be told, most of the time, I was scared as a porcupine giving birth. It felt like a ten-hour anxiety attack as I tried to get there as fast as I could while (somewhat) obeying the traffic laws of another country. And when I did get to Tonawanda, I had two dollars left, zero nerves and I couldn't even cry when I saw my husband. He was leaning against the car, arms crossed, relaxed, smiling and full of pride. He looked like a commercial. I, on the other hand, was as white as Wonder Bread (and quite possibly the people of northern New York State?), knees wobbling together like Bambi's first steps and as clammy as my clam. I looked like a warning sign. I think I was suffering from post-traumatic stress or something. We finally got home at 10:00 p.m. Just a few blocks from our house, we had to stop at the railway for a train to go by. *Planes, trains and automobiles*, I thought before asking my husband if there was any wine in the fridge.

Making heads or tails of it

So what did this whole thing mean and what did it teach me? Well, I'm still gleaning lessons from it more than two years later, but I think what it meant for me was trust. Trust in my GPS and trust in the GPS of the Universe. It might not give us the easiest way to get there or the straightest line, but it will get us there in the safest way that's meant for us. And in a way that's for our highest and greatest good.

After my husband and I crossed the Canadian border, I saw a rainbow. The arc covenant and then, I swear to God, I saw the most astonishing, remarkable sight. I would've thought I was hallucinating if my husband hadn't seen it too. We saw, in the golden sky, as the sun was setting, clouds shaped in an image of Jesus's face. I'm serious. It was obvious and plain as day, and now I'm part of that clan of people who have seen saints and godly figures in their toast and latte froth. It was Jesus! It was unbelievable. It was so detailed! And I believe it was planted there to show me that it's okay. The Universe has got me: "I'm here. You're safe and you are loved. I will always get you home safely."

It's funny, at that conference that weekend we heard from Mike Dooley, author and speaker who coined the phrase, "Thoughts become things." He likened the way of the Universe to a GPS system. He said you don't need to know how you're going to get there. That's for the GPS or Universe to figure out. You just need to plug in where you want to go and put the pedal to the medal and soon enough, one way or another, even if you take the wrong turn, the Universe will re-route and guide you. But it's contingent on *action*.

I don't know what would've happened if I hadn't decided to drive home from Philadelphia. I supposed I could've spent another couple days checking out the city and waiting to go home. But that didn't feel very empowering to me. I would've likely felt put out and in victim mode again, waiting on external forces to take me to where I wanted to go. Doing this on my own, just me, the Appalachian Mountains, my phone GPS and more tollbooths than I could count, made me stronger. It made me realize, once again, that I'm capable of great things.

I remember learning that lesson after I gave birth to my children: *My body just did whaaat??* but I guess, like labour pains, we sometimes forget that important stuff. Women are so strong, and yet it shows up in such a different way than how men demonstrate strength. The Universe needs to remind us sometimes just how strong we are, just how much we can do and endure when we partner with grace and let the Divine guide us home.

I also learned that I didn't need to be rescued—even by my husband. I was capable of rescuing myself. And I did! I learned that I was resourceful. I got home on sixty dollars. And I didn't need to always see the full picture because my instincts were good. My resilience muscle got a good workout on that trip and one very important reinforcement I received is one of the sayings that annoys me the most, but it's so true: "It's all about the journey." And as Anatole France once said, "If the path be beautiful, let us not ask where it leads."

A series of small steps

That weekend in Chicago, Mike Dooley encouraged us to just do *something*. Do something to take action and move in the direction of your dreams. He said to make a list of all the actions you could take to move in the direction of what you want and then just pick one or a few. "Pick the least suckiest path," he said. "Just like when you use an actual GPS system, you plug in where you want to go but then you can't just leave the car in park or you won't get anywhere," he said. "You need to move and the Universe will adjust and re-route if needed to help you reach where you envisioned yourself going." It's that leap of faith that will get you there. It's about believing there's a safety net below you even though you can't see it or know it's there for sure. Maybe you'll fall, right? But what if you don't. It takes courage and faith to believe that things will turn out right, even if you *do* fall. Because that fall will be rich in lessons and your healing journey may take you to the exact place you needed to go. The Divine has your back. Good always wins and in the end (beginning and middle for that matter), it's all going to be okay.

It reminds me of Newton's First Law of Motion: "Every object in a state of uniform motion tends to remain in that state of motion unless an external force is applied to it." It's one of the most painfully simple ideas that can't be repeated enough. Without taking action, you will not get anywhere. Do something. Do anything that makes sense to you. Motion beats inertia. Try something out. Try something different. Ask the Universe to guide you.

This is what happened to the Wright brothers back in 1903. They beat out corporations in the race to build a working plane because they emphasized action over planning, which we sometimes must do. Take it from a girl who's developed hundreds of strategic plans for corporations over the course of her career—sometimes we get too stalled in the planning. After a failed flight, the Wright brothers would go back to their workshop and make a small, cheap and quick adjustment and then they'd test the plane again. This was in contrast to the corporations that would spend months of planning and massive sums of money before trying another flight. The Wright brothers were nimble and they didn't have to fight red tape. They were credited with inventing, building and flying the first successful airplane because they took action. Their well-financed competitors lost because they tried to predict everything and create a perfect plan. This idea has spread fast to Silicon Valley and beyond because of books like Eric Ries's *The Lean Startup*. It's all about having a vision, steering and accelerating. Eric says he's come to believe that learning is the essential unit of progress for startups. "The effort that is not absolutely necessary for learning what customers want can be eliminated. I call this validated learning because it is always demonstrated by positive improvements in the startup's core metrics."[49]

In fact, a lot of corporations today are taking a lesson from this entrepreneurial spirit. When I was in financial services, we were introducing the *'Lean Six Sigma Methodology'* through our global operations, which relied on a collaborative effort to improve performance by systematically removing waste. It's about being in that continuous improvement state of mind, mining for golden opportunities to improve and then just doing it. Trying out something new and if it doesn't work, meh – we'll try something else out. I remember the faces of some of the people I was working with when we were trying to get these new ideas off the ground. It was radically different from the risk-averse, belts-and-suspenders kind of MO we were used to working within. But it garnered some truly remarkable savings and results, all from taking action and trying something on to see if it fits. Imagine!

It reminds me of the brand Nike—named after the Goddess of Victory herself, by the way—and its famous slogan, "Just Do It." Alanis Morissette did it with her highly acclaimed album *Jagged Little Pill* (that won five Grammy's including 'Album of the Year' in 1995), which she wrote in 45 minutes! Sylvester Stallone did it with *Rocky*. He had $106.00 in the bank, his wife was pregnant, his dog was starving, he couldn't get an acting job nor could he pay the rent on his seedy Hollywood apartment. And that's when he took action. He sat down and wrote the screenplay for *Rocky* in three and a half days and sold it to producers Irwin Winkler and Robert Chartoff on the condition that he would play *Rocky*. They persuaded someone to film it on the shoestring budget of one million dollars, which they did in twenty-eight days and the result? Well, you know the result. The 1976 movie *Rocky* grossed over two hundred million at the box office. *Rocky* won three Oscars: Best Picture, Best Director and Best Film Editing. It also earned Sylvester Stallone an Academy Award nomination for Best Actor. And today, Stallone's films have grossed over $3.5 billion, making him one of the biggest movie stars of all time. A total guy's guy but something to learn here! We've all heard lots of stories about taking action and the power that comes of it. It's about having an almost un-goddess-like work ethic. But...what I haven't mentioned yet is that there's a very important balance to maintain.

Receiving

Action is a masculine energy. Earlier in the book I talked about how women are the chalice, the receptacle of light to be filled with the Divine Feminine energy. To make ultimate use of the chalice, it's about emptying out what is no longer serving us (and consequently others) so we can be a receptacle for the Divine to fill us, work through us, spill over us so we can spill her goodness onto others. It depends on us being willing to receive and accept what is unfolding for us and gratefully embracing what is being sent our way. This is where the balance lies. We've talked a lot about taking action, doing, getting, hunting down, controlling and making it happen. But too much emphasis on this action can tip the scales into the yang masculine energy versus the yin, which is a softer, moon-based energy that doesn't seek but sits open and ready, like the lotus flower, to receive. It's an energy that understands its role (and power) in allowing the energy and flow of life to happen.

So on that trip from Chicago to Philadelphia to Tonawanda to Waterloo, I was also offered blessings to receive. Elya was a blessing. The Universe sent me The Little Mermaid when I needed her most. Do you know the symbolism of a mermaid? I always look these things up on sites like whats-your-sign.com when animals, nature or symbols cross my path because I see them as messages from the Universe. A mermaid means love, seeing beauty, untamed, femininity, persuasion and perception. They are often associated with love goddesses such as Aphrodite and Venus. They symbolize feminine (yin) power! They also represent wild freedom, rebellious spirits and ferocious independence. Thank you, Universe! What else did I need to receive? That despite me feeling like sixty dollars wasn't enough (the not enough web I so often get myself caught in), everything was enough. I had enough. I was enough to get myself through the journey. I just needed to relax, trust and have faith that while I was doing my part, the Universe had the GPS and and the wheel. I also could've had more fun with the whole adventure but more on that later.

Both acting and receiving are powerful energies that are needed to ebb and flow through life. There are different seasons and times for these energies to take centre stage. Right now, for me, the time is about the Divine Feminine. She's coaxing me into receiving, letting go of resistance (remember my hand on the steering wheel?), opening my heart and encouraging me to stay softer, more fluid and in an easy state. After years of burning the candle at both ends and working, working, working and proving, proving, proving and achieving, achieving, achieving (despite feeling unfulfilled), she is showing me what surrender and acceptance feel like and for the first time in my life, when I'm practicing these principles, I am truly learning and living balance.

Sipping from her cup

We are receptacles. We are all chalices for Divine love and light. These Divine energies of love and light are the essence of all spiritual qualities like peace, harmony, goodness, healing, and wisdom. So be open to receiving them. We must receive them first before we can radiate them out. It's as simple as allowing them in and accepting what is given. Over the years, I've made that hard because I've resisted it, and, as we know, what resists persists. Divine light and love are already there for us but often obscured by thinking, doubt, worry, resentment and all the usual suspects found within the conglomeration of the ego. So in a sense, receiving is actually an awakening or recognition of the light and love already here. It's a matter of dropping the veils.

CHAPTER 7 Reflections:

1. When have you taken action—and a leap of faith—without knowing how it would turn out?
2. If you could plug in any destination into a magical GPS that would take you anywhere in life (beyond and including a geographic location), where would your heart want to go? What are five actions you can take to move you closer to that destination?
3. When was the last time you graciously received something? How did you feel about it?
4. Describe a time (or times) when you felt that you alone—standing still with your socks on (or barefooted)—was enough.

8
Have Faith

> "Be faithful in small things because it is in them that your strength lies."
>
> ~ MOTHER TERESA

"Have a little faith." Has anyone ever said this to you? Maybe it came at a time of uncertainty, a time when you couldn't predict the results. You might have felt lost or in a dreaded place of waiting. Maybe you needed comforting. It takes faith to believe those four little words have enough juice to influence an outcome.

It took a little faith for me to write this chapter. For other chapters (once I got started!), the words and imagery flowed easily to and from me. The stories I picked up along my journey seemed to dance into this seamless connection, and I felt like divinity was flowing through me, increasing my confidence and allowing me to deliver those words with passion, my truth and grace.

Sitting down to write this chapter was anything but easy. I read and re-read it and while some of the words glimmered on the page, I still didn't know how to piece them all together. Were other chapters beginner's luck? Could I do this again? Would I feel like an imposture talking about this topic? Would you read my words? Would I have something meaningful to offer you? I had my doubts.

But in addition to the Mother Teresa quote at the beginning of this chapter, I came across a gospel reading about faith. It was literally one of those crack-the-Bible-open-and-point-to-a-passage moments. While I felt a little silly doing it, I made a choice to honour the idea that popped into my head. I got out of my own way and trusted these were the words I needed to hear in that moment. In the passage, Luke asked God to make his faith greater. God replied, "If you had faith as big as a mustard seed, you could say to this mulberry tree, 'Pull yourself up by the roots and plant yourself in the sea!' and it would obey you."

When I read that, coupled with the Mother Teresa quote, it reminded me of two things. The first was my son's baptism in 2009. The gospel reading that day talked about Jesus' parable of the mustard seed, how it was the smallest seed in the world and at night, when the farmer slept, it sprouted and grew into the biggest plant of all. The Kingdom of God is like this, Jesus said.

I remembered going out for lunch with our family after the baptismal ceremony. I was so full of joy that day. I recall raising a glass to a room filled with family and friends (No, I didn't cheers to my vagina that day although if there were ever a day to commemorate the performance of that brilliant body part *alone*, that would have been an occasion to do so!). Instead, I toasted, "To Everett, my little mustard seed, as he sets out on his faith journey." That image of a mustard seed was so powerful and ironic. The road to parenthood wasn't easy for us; it was paved with a lot of heartache and devastation. For me, rock bottom hit on Christmas Eve 2007 when all that I had left, after three miscarriages, was "a very little faith." In fact, if I could've measured my faith then, it would've been about the size of a little mustard seed. Maybe smaller. That's all I could *muster* at the time.

But over the weeks and months and years that followed, that seed of faith took root and grew, sprouting and transforming into the beautiful eight-year-old Everett Zion I have the honour of mothering today. His name means strength and it shows. I believe it was him trying to come through each of those bodies; the first three just weren't made for the life he chose to lead. Only the last. That was a strong body to match the strength of his spirit. He was 7 lbs. 5 oz. when he was born—skinny, long and all arms and legs, but he was *strong*. He was strong enough to endure thirty-three hours of labour with me, and he holds a quiet strength within him today. He is truly a gift and if I hadn't accepted faith into my life, he would not have been born. But it's interesting how quickly we can forget—I can forget—these astonishing reference points when we're going through a crisis. Like the next one I was about to face.

Just after Everett turned one year old, we found out we were pregnant again. I was so happy things took this time, and so quickly, but was also scared about everything being okay. The first trimester had always been scary for me. And then one day, I felt like my worst fears were being realized. I started bleeding again. I immediately made an appointment with the doctor. They did some blood work and said my hormone levels were low. I got the sense from their facial expressions that things weren't looking good. I had to go and get more blood work done every few days to see how much the levels were changing. Agony. The waiting. The worry. I thought it would be best for me to protect myself by starting to prepare for the worst. I chose to stay numb throughout those long days. My hormone counts didn't seem to be rising quickly enough. I was bracing for the worst. I didn't even want to think about my faith, or what happened with Everett.

Beginners luck. I started to doubt. *You got your miracle, and miracles don't grow on trees*, I told myself. I even went into a self-badgering (instead of loving) place of, *You get what you get and don't get upset*. Let's just say it was not the positive self-talk I practice most of the time today. By the time I went to the doctor's office to get the final results, I was downright pissed off. I was still bleeding. Things weren't looking good. I was fearful of another D&C like I had to have after one of the other miscarriages that had gone further along. I just felt stuck in this cycle of pain. I didn't even realize the words that flew out of my mouth at the time until I said them, but when I went up to the counter to check-in with reception, I told them my name and said that I was here for the miscarriage.

The doctor came into the examining room all chipper, which pissed me off even more (*Do your homework!* I thought. *Don't you know you're coming into the room of a women who's suffered not one, not two, but four fucking miscarriages?! Show some compassion! Or match my mood or something!*). The judgments, I know. But I was distraught. "Okay!" he said with a smile on his face. "So we're all set and things are looking good." *Wait. What?* "I'm here for the miscarriage," I said for the second time. Again, the words just kept flying out of my mouth. "No, everything looks great," he said. "Your hormone levels have taken a big turn upwards and everything is happening at the normal levels now. A bit of spotting—let's keep an eye on that, but everything looks good from my perspective." I was dumbfounded.

And so twenty-one months after Everett was born, we were doubly blessed with Georgia Trinity after another shaky first trimester and a birthing experience where everything went wrong before it was right. But grace got us through it. Again, she came to us like a dream's dream, far more wonderful than we could've ever imagined. And once again, I was reminded that with a little faith, anything is possible. Cue the George Michael song! From then on, I made it a point to remember these moments of faith. I hold them close like a security blanket when I need them. Like little beacons of light, they have become reference points to remind me that anything is possible: *Look at the beautiful, smart, loving, kind, funny, glorious children I get to mother today; they came to me through faith and grace.*

And just a side note, the other ironic thing is that during my rock bottom before becoming pregnant with Everett, I remember lamenting to God. Oh, I was mad. I was pissed, in fact. Thank goodness I had Pastor Doug, a very down-to-earth minister who told me to go ahead and get angry at God because God wasn't human and could handle my anger. "Go throw crucifixes in the Avon River if it makes you feel better," he said to me with compassion as we sat over our emptied coffee cups at Balzac's. I love that man. And I love his wife, Sharon. She is the brilliant powerhouse who fuels him. I took his advice (not about the crucifixes—the river was frozen over at the time—but about letting the anger rise up and out of me).

Psalm 130 confirms this with, "Out of the depths I cry to you, O Lord".[50] Essentially, it's a euphemism for "Fuck, please listen to me God!" Certainly God can take our anger and anger can be healing if we eventually move from its grip. Naming it allows that to happen on the road to healing.

One of the things I yelled out loud into thin air was that I just wanted to be able to experience joy and laugh again. And when was Everett born? April Fool's Day. Just like in Genesis when Sarai laughed at the thought of Abraham and her having a child when she was ninety and he was one hundred. Can you imagine? Even through the grace of God, it seemed impossible. But it *was* possible, and they had a son named Isaac, which is Hebrew for 'laughter.' It's like Sarah and I have these markers, these breadcrumbs that lead us back to our faith journey.

Now, I don't mean to oversimplify what happened with me or what could be happening with you. I'm speeding up the story and potentially downplaying the devastation at the time when I didn't know how things would work out. Medical challenges, physical limitations and deaths are hard to make sense or receive comfort from even through a faith lens. There was a point in my journey when I didn't know where or how things were going to go. Another thing Pastor Doug helped me realize was that my deepest desire wasn't to become pregnant: my deepest desire was to become a mother. His words were reassuring when he said to Robert and me, "Some way, some how, you will become parents and one day I will be putting water on a kid's head." The visual of a baptism celebration gave me hope. And it made me think of that anonymous saying about God's three answers to our prayers: yes, not yet, or I have something better in mind.

Faith doesn't always give us what we want, but it gets us through our brightest days and our darkest hours, even when the path seems unclear, the page is blank, it's just a flat square field without any forecast of rain. Sometimes we're faced with a modern-day Egyptian desert like the one the Israelites found themselves in, and I must say those forty years in the desert got a bad rap. Yes, the Israelites were lost and felt ignored and aimless without direction or purpose, but they were fed. Every day. With manna and companionship and they were cared for by God. And once they were strengthened, grew a relationship with the Divine and surrendered—allowing the little faith they had to take root and grow—they were led out of the desert and into the Promised Land. I was fed too and needed to surrender before I could be delivered. Before I could, quite literally, deliver Everett and Georgia.

Sometimes we can't see the whole picture. We think we can see a clear beginning and end, but we can't. Only God, the Universe, Source, the Divine—however you describe its being—can see. This life isn't even as clearly carved out as we may think—with its beginning at birth and ending at death—we don't know the whole picture yet. It's why we need to have faith, even in times when we feel lost and like we've been forsaken, because God is leading us through a path that will end in glory. We just need a little faith to get there.

Faith and trust. In many ways, they're one in the same. And it's called "blind faith" for a reason. Many times—I'd argue from personal experience that *most* of the time—we don't know where we're going or where we're being led. But we *are* being led if we've asked to be. And just like the Israelites, we will be led to the Promised Land. There are too many similarities between us modern-day people and the Israelites to ignore our lineage and this repeated pattern over time. Just like them, we can get caught up in our own faith-doubt cycles, but we just need to look back at those teachings to help us *see* the road ahead and envision the Promised Land to come.

What do you think could happen if you took a leap of faith and trusted in God's care and timing?

In the Kingdom (Queendom?) of God, each of us is a mustard seed. At times, the work we do or even the people we *are* might seem trite or insignificant, too small to have impact. But we are anything but small because we are divinely made. The seed within our seed is God's mothering and fathering love for us, and knowing that and trusting the process, the plan and timing will allow us to blossom together into the most colossal and beautiful field of glory, beyond what we could ever imagine.

The garden of life

In many ways, having faith is just like letting go and letting nature run its course. Allowing that tiny little mustard seed to transform into something incredible. Three springs ago, I planted my first vegetable garden, something I had been dreaming of for years. I used to write a blog about local food, and one of my readers asked me to join a committee in Stratford that supported the slow food movement. Can you imagine? Slow food. This was something that sounded almost foreign in a world that has become so defined by speed. We're used to fast cars, planes, athletes, super-computers, rides, technology—and especially fast results. But the International Slow Food Movement turns all of that on its head.

Instead, it envisions a world where everyone can access and enjoy food that's good for them, good for those who grow it and good for the planet. And that takes time. The organization is guided by three principles: good, clean and fair.

Now, I'm a girl who values *the real deal*. Offer me genuine, salt-of-the-earth things and I'm there. So I started attending events where area farmers would partner with local chefs and create the most sublime dishes—handmade; from scratch; born from a place of deep love and respect for the land, the elements, the creatures and the care that went into cultivating and harvesting that nourishing food. And there was a love that went into preparing it in such a way that would bring out the best in them, along with nature's bounty. It was done so in a way that would offer reciprocity through sustainable practices for all the land had given.

It just amazed and inspired me. I'd witness these farmers who would show me their soil-stained hands cupping the most stunning vegetables. I mean, beets that looked like *jewels*. And the sense of pride that filled the sun-kissed creases of their humble faces? It was beautiful.

After witnessing this magic, I was hooked, and started dreaming of a day when I'd have my own vegetable garden where I too could enjoy the fruits (and vegetables) of my labour, respecting and appreciating the simple things in life that mean so much.

I just didn't think it was really possible.

For a few reasons. One: I didn't consider myself a gardener. At all. Up until that point, I killed my kids' chia pets. And house plants? They didn't stand a chance. Fresh-cut flowers would just keel over and wilt at the sight of me. So I questioned my ability to take on this project, and even if I did, where would I put it? Our backyard wasn't big enough and the previous owner had already landscaped it. There was a small patch of land where the kids would run around, and I didn't want to put a vegetable garden smack in the middle of it. I got stuck in the *hows*, not knowing how this whole thing would take shape. Sounded great on paper but doubt started creeping in.

I also didn't know if I'd have the time to take care of it. Life was busy with kids and jobs and hockey and swimming lessons. Would I be able to water as often as I needed to and tend to the weeds and feed it the nutrients it needed to survive and thrive? And I guess the biggest obstacle of all—what was at the root of all of these excuses—was that thing I was resisting most: fear.

It's that fear thing again! Fear of failure, fear of putting in a lot and not getting as much or maybe even any of it in return. I resisted the feeling of failure. Oh, how I hated that feeling. And every time I failed, I made up a new set of rules in my mind for how to avoid going back to that place. If I do this, this and this, I won't have to go back there, which often meant "playing it safe." Hanging out at the sidelines. Helping other people thrive when I secretly wished it was me up there too. And that's dangerous territory for me because sometimes, in the blink of an eye, it's easy to end up in a place of resentment.

So, I set it aside for a while until one day, a lightning called 'clarity' struck me.

It was a sunny Sunday afternoon. I was feeling pretty carefree that day, enjoying the weather, hearing the birds, talking with my wonderful husband, laughing and dreaming together over a glass of wine. And that's when it hit me: I could use that little strip of land at the side of our house to make a long and narrow raised bed to house a vegetable garden. I ran out there with measuring tape and giddy with excitement. I measured the spot and noticed it receives a lot of sunshine throughout the day. It was something I hadn't even considered before and it felt...genius!

And then another idea came to me. My brother-in-law is a landscaper. I could pay him to come and build a raised wooden bed for me. A few minutes later, we connected by phone and he was thrilled to take on the job. It was all happening so easily and seamlessly and fast. What was going on? It was so awesome!

And then, the most miraculous thing happened: I started debunking my fears. Oh sure, they drifted back one by one, but like a game of table tennis, I popped them right back onto doubt's side of the net. So I didn't know how to plant a vegetable garden and had only killed chia pets and houseplants up until that point. So what! I had a square-foot-gardening book and I had Google. That's a pretty good start. So I didn't have a lot of extra time. This could be an outlet, a family project. A new hobby. Maybe even a stress reliever! I could teach my kids about where food comes from. I could quite literally teach them that you reap what you sow. And little did I know that this vegetable garden was about to teach me some powerful lessons about life, love and faith.

I began to watch my words. I stopped telling people about how I had only killed plants up until that time because I didn't want to feed on that energy any more. I decided to release those limiting beliefs. Instead, I humbly spoke about the facts, my passion and the things that were working in my favour to get me there.

I stopped boxing myself in. I used my resources. I hadn't even thought of my brother-in-law's support up until that time. In the past, I struggled with asking for help, feeling not worthy of *the ask*, fearing rejection or something. But I put those aside and asked for what I needed. And lo and behold, a helping hand extended. Just like that.

I went into planning mode. Planning is part of my job, so this part came easily to me. Oh, I can whip up a plan pretty quickly, and I had charts and diagrams and notebooks and schedules to get me there from early to late harvest. What did I struggle with? I struggled with what would happen after all the planning was done.

I would have to wait.

After all the planning and planting and watering and digging and labelling and testing the soil and adjusting it with natural materials such as eggs shells to promote nutrients and growth. Because you know, good soil is so important. And after all that was taken care of, after the sun was setting and my back was hurting and my nails were lined with dirt, I thought I'd look at that long and narrow vegetable garden, take a deep breath and exhale a sense of pride knowing I had given it my all.

But it didn't quite happen that way.

Sure, I was glad I had followed my own explicit set of instructions. That was true. But instead of feeling pride and relief, I felt anxiety creep in. I started second-guessing myself about what I had done and if I had done it correctly. I retraced and reviewed my steps and only after a while did I realize that no, I had indeed done all that I set out to do. That's not what this was about.

This was about letting go. Having faith.

The *doing* part was over. Now I had to step back, take a breath and just *be*.

There was nothing more to do. In fact, even when I tried to force make-work projects to care and tend for that garden, it backfired. Did you know that dill doesn't like you to fuss over it too much when it's first planted? I read somewhere that it "sulks" if you do this because it just wants to get its roots in there and accustomed to its new environment. It just needed to be. It needed me to let it be. And so that was the next lesson – and possibly – the hardest lesson that beautiful stretch of dirt taught me: to let go, let the Universe do its thing and have faith.

I found this both easy and difficult depending on the time of day. There were times throughout the day when I'd walk by the stretch of dirt and dream about it blossoming into beautiful and bountiful vegetables to nourish my family. And then, sometimes just hours later, I could walk by and doubt, thinking: *What if it doesn't grow a thing? What if my seeds won't sprout? What if I did it wrong? What if...* Same-day thinking. I'm reminded of the whole faith-doubt cycle the Israelites went through during their forty years in the desert. They'd spend their days walking the unfruitful blanket of desert sand wrought with fear and doubt about their own survival. But some way or another, they would be fed and find solace in sleep before waking to a new day.

For me, faith has always been the hardest lesson. Because I question things—so many things: *Does the Divine really see me? Like really? My troubles aren't deep and there are others who are far worse off than me. I have first-world problems. Is there time, space or energy to help little ol' me with something like my little ol' vegetable garden?*

Again, I put the thoughts aside until I pulled out a package of seeds and realized that I too am like those tiny little seeds (shaped like the vesica piscis!) in my hand. And what is the gentle force that initiates their growth? What I know for sure is that it's a force far greater than me. Far greater than sun, soil and water. And eventually, after many days of dormancy, something made those tiny seeds grow. Call it what you will—God, the Universe, Source, Alpha and Omega, Divinity, Yahweh, Allah, Krishna, Creator, Great Spirit—it's all the same. And it permeates everything: this energy is found in the water, the soil, the sunshine, the insects. It is all around and helping those delicate seeds grow just like the elements around me are helping me grow into all I was meant to be.

The sight of those tiny seeds in my hand again reminded me of Everett's baptism. When Pastor Doug Reble spoke of the mustard seed parable, he described a farmer who reached into his seed pack and tried to pull out one golden mustard seed, which was quite a trick to get just one because they were so tiny. You practically need bifocals to see one seed. A small handful looks like finely ground pepper. It's amazing that such a tiny seed grows into such a large bush. A large sparrow, that has to pick hundreds of tiny seeds just for its breakfast, can sit comfortably on its sturdy branches. And it would grow whether the farmer worried about it or not.

There are some things in life that are certain. Jesus says the Kingdom of God is one of them. Our job is to plant the seeds of the Kingdom (Queendom?) and then trust God to bring in the harvest. Trust is key and something I had to do as my belly grew with my son and daughter. It was something I had to do even with my little 'ol vegetable garden. Trust is a muscle I'm trying to strengthen more and more each day.

With very small things and a little trust, God can do some very big things. With Moses's rod, God divided the sea. With David's slingshot and stone, great Goliath was defeated. A small boy donated five loaves and two fish, and five thousand people were fed. A poor woman put two pennies in the treasury and received the highest praise. When a baby is born, I can't help but think of the great things God will do with that little child.

God is still bringing in the Kingdom, and maybe the Queendom, through small, through people like my son and daughter, through those tiny seeds in the garden and through people like you and me. Oh yes, I know we get discouraged. We think our small contribution to world hunger won't make a difference. Pastor Doug reminds us that we are victims of bigness. We have mega malls, mega sales, mega churches and mega storms. In contrast, Jesus spoke of the importance of small things: a mustard seed, a cup of cold water, a widow's mite, a kindness done to the least of these. Jesus knows we often forget. Mary does too. The size of the bush, the healthy spread of branches depends on the vitality of the seed.

Know how much God trusts us, with unshakeable confidence, to go on planting the seeds through a mother's prayer, a father's encouragement, a little girl's joy, a young boy's imagination. It's about trusting the Universe to bring in the harvest by continuing to plant the seeds of the kingdom (queendom?) in our own small ways and sleep well. Leave the outcome in God's hands and God will bring in the harvest beyond anyone's guess.

And it happened, not just with our son who came like rainbow at the end of a road of numerous disappointments and heartache, perseverance, blind faith and love, but also with our daughter, twenty-one months later, after what we thought was another miscarriage and after an emergency C-section where everything seemed to go wrong before it went unbelievably right.

These didn't happen in my time, but they happened in the Divine's time. And I've come to learn and trust that my time isn't always God's time, and sometimes there are even bigger things in store. Beyond what I thought could be possible.

And so, when I allow myself to move into this place of love and trust, my fears start to dissipate. I've come to know that the opposite of love is not hate: it's fear. And so I choose to go to a place of love when I find myself treading into the darkness. It's okay to hang out in the shadows once in a while because its contrast can remind us of the power of light.

When my vegetable garden started growing, it brought me so much joy. It was such a treat and lesson to show my kids what can grow from the tiniest seed. It taught me faith and trust, and it allowed me to teach my children through a very real and vivid example. It taught me that I don't need to worry because a power much greater than me is working through those seeds and will bring them into radiant, abundant being and that fear and perception of lack are not helpful. It taught me to trust that abundance is not only possible, it is a universal law. It has already happened and there's evidence of it everywhere. Remember the mustard seed and the rolling yellow hills.

It reminded me of the love that went into the meals that the best farmers and chefs prepare, that secret ingredient—love. As I used my finger to cover each seed with a little dirt, I blessed each one and told it I loved it. Because that is how so many wonderful things are grown in this world. Through seeds of love.

And the rest I'm sure is no surprised. My first vegetable garden grew with vigour and strength and vitality and love. It blossomed into a sight that attracted people in our neighbourhood to walk by, stop and admire its beauty. So many kind words, compliments and much neighbourly love was shared. It inspired some to grow gardens of their own. It connected us. And we shared the abundant harvests with our neighbours—we had so much beautiful produce. It tasted so sweet and delicious. We're onto our third year with the garden now and it's even stronger, bolder and more beautiful. Who knew?

That's how the Kingdom or Queendom of God works, and when we get the lesson, it can happen in record time. We grow and all become whole through the tiniest seeds of faith. And as Lao Tzu once said, "Nature never hurries, and yet everything is accomplished."

CHAPTER 8 Reflections:

1. Where in your life do you need to have a little faith? What feels impossible right now?
2. What are you trying to control based on what you want, possibly ignoring the greater things the Divine has in store for you?
3. Have you asked to be led by a higher power?
4. Is there a relationship you've been struggling with? Is there an occupation you'd love to explore but feel it's an impossible dream? Is there a way you could serve your community that makes you afraid—maybe you don't feel good enough or you might be concerned with what others might think? Is there someone you want to reach out to but you don't know how or what to say or do (even though you might not need to say or do anything but show up)?
5. Is there a death, illness or limitation you're trying to make sense of that God could help you through?

9
Accept and Love Yourself, Girl!

"You can search throughout the entire universe for someone who is more deserving of your love and affection than you are yourself, and that person is not to be found anywhere. You, yourself, as much as anybody in the entire universe, deserve your love and affection."

~ GAUTAMA BUDDHA

In 1992, a song hit the radio charts by a band named Blind Melon. Do you remember *"No Rain?"* It was one of those catchy little songs that stuck in your head and rolled off your tongue. But I think what *really* made this song reach its multi-platinum status was its video.

If you've ever seen the video, you'll remember the main character. She was such a vivid image. Affectionately dubbed "The Bee Girl," this nine-year-old youngster appears on stage in the opening scene wearing a homemade bumblebee costume and a yellow pipe-cleaner heart crown. Her red hair was braided in pigtails, she had oversized black-framed glasses, a yellow-and-black striped bodice, frilly tutu and shiny black tap shoes. She bumbles around the stage leaping, posing, spinning and sharing a tap routine that's uniquely her own. Yet with each step, she appears more and more self-conscious as she dances before the dark audience.

Eventually, at the end of her routine, that dark audience makes itself known with a few out-of-synch claps and an eruption of taunting laughter. The Bee Girl covers her face in shame and runs off stage in tears.

The music cues, the video plays on, revealing a story of this hurt and weary little bumble bee, who wanders through the city, stopping various people along the way to perform her tap-dance routine, yearning to be understood by someone and ultimately *accepted*.

And then, at the point in the song where the word "escape" is repeated, the little bumble bee discovers an iron gate in the middle of a beautiful field, and peeks through the bars to find, to her astonishment, a group of "bee people" (her team!) of all shapes and sizes dancing joyfully, just like her, in the lush green field. She is overjoyed and just rocks out, freely basking in her own bliss, being who she really is and being accepted by those around her.

I can relate to this little bee girl, and I'm sure many of you can too because at the core of the human condition, we all just want to be accepted. And for many of us, without even realizing it, that becomes an ongoing and very much external process. We look to be accepted by our friends and social groups. We look to be accepted by our sports teams and leisure circles. We look to be accepted by our parents and within our families. For some, this is a life-long pursuit. We look to be accepted in our workplaces and by our bosses, neighbours and communities, our churches and the groups within them. We look to be accepted by our cultures and those who share our gender. Sometimes our past, certainly our present, and often we even worry about future acceptance: Will our children be accepted? Will our grandchildren be accepted? And then there's the root. *Self*-acceptance. Will we ever fully and completely accept ourselves, just as we are today, at our current weight, health, age, job title, salary bracket, purpose in life—the people we are? There is so much acceptance seeking out there; it's almost become the norm. Just ask the advertising industry. Advertisers make millions capitalizing on our need to feel accepted by exposing our feelings of inadequacy and unworthiness.

Yet our true maker, Mother and Father, Divine Spirit, Source—God—has a love that will truly quench our souls if we allow it to. And once our souls are quenched, we can accept and love ourselves deeply so we can love and accept others freely.

For me, self-love and self-acceptance led to the need for some real reconciliation in my life. And I don't mean reconciling with another person. I mean reconciling with *myself.* There were times when I felt like I was living a double life. I worked in a job where I was known for my professionalism and polish. My suits were as stiff as my demeanor. I was strict with myself, had high expectations of others, and struggled with viewing vulnerability as weakness, when in fact nothing could be farther from the truth.

Even writing this book caused reconciliation within me. I worked in public relations, marketing and communications throughout most of my career. I know how to script refined key messages to promote confidence and instill trust in our investors and clients. I know how to market products that help customers achieve lifetime financial security while building and protecting the overall brand.

And suddenly, I'm writing a book that references vaginas all over the place. In fact, as you've read, I start the whole thing off talking about my own vagina, how I toasted it on my twenty-sixth birthday and how I think vaginas are truly awe-inspiring, miraculous and beautiful. My East Indian father, the Punjabi community, members of my family, what will they think? Will they understand or frown at my message? How will this impact how I have been viewed and known personally and professionally up until now? Will my friends cheer while my colleagues gawk in horror? What will my kids think when they reach an age where they'll understand what I'm putting into print? Will they be embarrassed? How will my mother-in-law deal with the small-town gossip mill that could ensue?

The truth is, I don't know and that's none of my business anyway. What I *do* know is that I've had a message burning in my heart for close to twenty years now, and my heart song needs to be released. This is who I really am and it's time to fully own and accept that. It's funny, I always try to pay attention to the signs of the Universe, and while I was writing this book (slowly, procrastinating over a long period of time), I went to see my naturopath because I had broken out in terrible acne, wasn't sleeping well, felt bloated and just wasn't quite myself. You know what he discovered? I had a buildup of estrogen coursing through my veins, and I needed some supplements to get rid of the surplus so I could re-balance my hormones and get back to being me. Ironic that I was procrastinating writing a book about the Divine Feminine and just needed to get it out of me? It's like I've been pregnant with this book for nineteen years. I even have pregnancy acne now! Thank Goddess I'm finally birthing it.

Loving the perfect imperfections

What took me many years to understand is a very simple piece of wisdom: wherever I go, I just need to be myself. That's all. I'm perfectly imperfect—and more than good enough—just the way I am. Reconciling who we are—our light and our dark and all the shades in between—helps us get closer to our maker. Accepting ourselves ignites our intrinsic divinity. It's like a beautiful statement to the Universe that says, "I see you. I acknowledge you. And I accept you as part of me. I am grateful that you are part of me." And it's met with a knowing that the Divine Spirit loves, honours and accepts us just as we are, no matter what.

There's a Hebrew word *poema* that sorta translates to 'little poem.' In God's eyes, we are like little *masterpieces*, these beautiful little poems spoken into life. Our response, in gratitude, is to create a reflection of God's image by the way we love and serve God and others. That starts by loving and accepting ourselves. How else can we truly be compassionate? And to live a life that glorifies the Divine.

Little Tanya

When I think of each of us being viewed, understood and treated like poetry God spoke into being, I am reminded of the Chris Morley poem entitled "To a Child." It goes like this:

The greatest poem ever known
Is one all poets have outgrown:
The poetry, innate, untold,
Of being only four years old.

Still young enough to be a part
Of Nature's great impulsive heart,
Born comrade of bird, beast, and tree
And unselfconscious as the bee-

And yet with lovely reason skilled
Each day new paradise to build;
Elate explorer of each sense,
Without dismay, without pretense!

In your unstained transparent eyes
There is no conscience, no surprise:
Life's queer conundrums you accept,
Your strange divinity still kept.

Being, that now absorbs you, all
Harmonious, unit, integral,
Will shred into perplexing bits,-
Oh, contradictions of the wits!

And Life, that sets all things in rhyme,
may make you poet, too, in time-
But there were days,
O tender elf,
When you were Poetry itself![51]

    Isn't that beautiful? It's important to go back, from time to time, to remind ourselves that we were once those tender elves. And in many ways, we still are because those children don't go away despite physical growth and the experiences we wrack up. Within us we still hold those inner children. Within us, we are every age we've ever been.

    It sometimes makes me sad when I think of that innocence and softness because as I grew, I became notoriously hard on myself. I know it, my friends know it, my teachers knew it and even my bosses know it too. It isn't something I liked about myself but it just felt like breathing. I didn't know when it started or stopped. It just was. And I guess it served me in some respects—I used to think it kept me motivated and on track with my goals. But over time, it had an erosive effect. Physically, it shot my adrenals. Like me, they were exhausted. It sucked my body's vitamin B stores dry. I felt "on" all the time, even in my sleep sometimes, which became disrupted. And the emotional strain was not good. My inner dialogue sounded just plain *mean* and what's worse, I didn't even notice it. It was just like this running loop in my head of judgments and not-good-enough thinking. I know where it originated but came to realize that it doesn't really matter. I took on the role of kicking my own ass as an adult, and I had choices so this was something within my realm of control now. It took me a few months of meditation to even start being aware of my own thinking, aware of passing thoughts, without judging them or at least being curious about them. *Wow. That was some kinda thought that just passed through my mind.* It was a time of just noticing the kind of thought traffic that would zip through my brain. And then, with more time, I came not to control those thoughts but realize they didn't have the power I once thought they did. They were just thoughts. They weren't me or divinity or my true self. They were just these things that would float on through, and if I didn't run after them, trying to chase or analyze them (oh, how I used to analyze them to try to understand the meaning), they would just float away. *Bye bye not-in-my-highest-good thought. See ya.* That was a major shift. It had like a Wizard of Oz effect on me. That voice wasn't all mighty, powerful and sought after, it was just some little man behind the curtain trying to get his needs met. Except the little man was my ego or my Gremlins. And that's okay. Actually, when I started to see that ego or Gremlin and look at it—shine a light on it—it shrunk in size and importance. Maybe it just likes to be paid attention to from time to time. That's okay. I can do that. It doesn't mean I'm going to engage in dialogue with it, make it feel a certain way or try to control it. I just take the Rick Carson approach and shine a light on that little fucker and let it go.

But after a while of being more aware and noticing things, I did start to observe some patterns or rhythms in my self-talk, and when I'd share it with my husband, he'd say, "Would you ever talk to Georgia that way? Would you ever be in the presence of someone who would talk to Georgia that way?" And the Mama Bear in me stretched out of my own skin. *I would never...how could I ever. If anyone EVER!* I thought to myself. While I couldn't imagine ever talking to my daughter that way, or my son, when I sat with it for a while, I found it sad that I would find it okay to talk to myself that way, to the little girl inside me that way, because she didn't disappear. She's still in there. The children we were are always inside of us. That was a realization for me as well. I just thought I grew up and needed to get on with things. I was an adult now. But no. I'm many different pieces and experiences. I'm a spiritual being who has seen and experienced many things in this life, and I believe in other lives too. So it was simple and complex at the same time. I had to honour that little girl who took on a lot of other people's shit at a young age. And I needed to hold her close and help heal her—heal myself.

My dear friend, Amy, is a healer in many ways. She's a registered massage therapist, reiki master, reflexologist, mother and angel, I'm convinced. She's like pure oxygen, really. You know one of those people who you just feel recharged to be around? That's Amy. Well, one night when I was on the massage table she was telling me about an exercise she had done for herself to help heal her inner child. She was at a retreat and the instructor was walking her through a guided meditation. You know one of those beautiful visual imagery ones where you're walking up a staircase and opening a door? Well, Amy found herself in her childhood home on a farm where she had grown up. She was about five years old and she was in a hallway crying. No one was around to comfort and console her. It's not to say they weren't in the house—they didn't physically abandon her—but they emotionally abandoned her because hugs and saying "I love you" and applications of comfort weren't offered in her house. In the meditation, Amy looked at her five-year-old self, bent down and gently wrapped her loving arms around her and let that sweet, innocent child cry onto her shoulder, rubbing her hair, sending her love, caring and wrapping her in loving kindness. It was a beautiful, poignant moment in her healing. As she was doing the meditation, although her eyes were closed, they were streaming tears and the instructor noticed. So she brought Amy a pillow to hug, like it was her five-year-old self. Like she was comforting and caring for her.

It might sound a little out there but it works. I tried it too. I did a guided meditation at home after hearing about this and I also put a childhood photo of myself beside me. I was about four years old when the photograph was taken. Cute as a button. Sweet and lovely. I'd look at Georgia the same way. And I visualized her. I visualized little Tanya, and I did the same thing. She wasn't crying but she was sad. She was hurting. She had taken on too much, something I was still doing as an adult. She needed a hug. She needed love and comforting. She needed to know that she was a child and didn't need to take on adult things. She's still inside me, and the adult who is inside me can take care of those things. She doesn't need to drive anymore or strive or achieve or to win affection. She can just be and she could help me by playing. As an adult it's like I've almost lost my ability to play. Even when my children were small, I'd play with them but I didn't enjoy it. It was time that I got some of that joy back.

Dark night of the soul

Many of us spend our whole lives avoiding the dark night of the soul because it means we'd need to allow all our grief to come up. All that stuff we've been stuffing down and avoiding or redirecting in ways that aren't honouring our true spirits or serving our souls. But allowing that stuff to come up is the start of the healing process. It involves trust, where the wounded child in us comes out of hiding and trusts that the adult us will be there to help her. It requires acceptance of what happened and the people who caused the pains, people who were likely wounded themselves. The grief process falls out of the shock of what we're uncovering and anger follows. While our logical minds might recognize that our parents did the best they could with what they had, there's also an awareness that the damage was more than skin deep. It could have been spiritually deep with life-damaging consequences. And that can stir up sadness, shame and loneliness. Just reading that may be enough to convince you to run the other way. But once you go through each of these steps, there's a clearing, a beautiful meadow on the other side. The rest of your life is just waiting for you to live and enjoy and not be burdened by the past. It's worth going through the process. We have to embrace, work through and release these feelings to come out healed and whole on the other side, filled with love for self.

It's not selfish to love ourselves. It's a necessary and continuous process to love and accept ourselves – just as we are – if we want to live a full, free life where we give back to others. Our chalice must be filled before it can spill onto those around us. You've heard that saying about love being a verb, well it's so true. It requires daily attention. Daily love. As the late Louise Hay said, "It clears us so we can love ourselves enough to love other people. And we can really help the planet when we come from a space of great love and joy on an individual basis. Love is the binding agent that holds the whole Universe together." It starts with self-love.

If you're like me, you might think this all sounds good on paper, but are asking, "How do I make it happen in my life in a real way that shows up and where I can see a difference over time?" Well, it's a series of small steps. It starts with deep appreciation for who you are, where you've come from and how it got you to where you are today. It's about looking in the mirror every morning and seeing all the different parts about you, or as Louise Hay reminded us, "...our little peculiarities, the embarrassments, the things we may not do so well, and all the wonderful qualities, too," and accepting them with loving eyes.

Recognizing self-love

I'm very much a learner on this journey. I haven't got it figured out by far. There's still so much to grow into (my own skin) and understand and admire and appreciate about myself. I know this in turn will do remarkable things for my relationships with others, which keeps me going. But what I've learned so far is that this being hard on myself thing that I've been carrying around with me for so long is like a blanket that covers up the light and beauty of what has already grown and developed within me. I didn't think I was doing very well at all in the self-love department until I stumbled across *The Six Pillars of Self-Esteem* by Nathanial Branden, which he describes as:

1. The practice of living consciously
2. The practice of self-acceptance
3. The practice of self-responsibility
4. The practice of self-assertiveness
5. The practice of living purposefully
6. The practice of personal integrity[52]

I love that the word *practice* precedes each of the pillars. As we're learning and growing and discovering, we need to practice these concepts until they become innate. While it sounded a bit odd to me, what I realized was that I needed to practice loving myself before I can get there automatically.

And another thing that dawned on me—what my coach helped me realize—was that I was already making great strides in each of these arenas. I was raising my consciousness and mindfulness by meditating every morning and having the courage to go down the path of coaching. I was being honest with myself and willing to look at all my *stuff*—the good, bad, light and dark, beauty marks and warts. There was amazing acceptance that had been bubbling up from these practices.

And self-responsibility? I had taken a week off work, unexpectedly, when I felt like I was fully dilated and I needed to go into labour with birthing this book. I made the choice and took action in a responsible way. I was practicing self-assertiveness—with *myself*. With my ego. Because let me tell you, there was lots of inner conflict going on. My soul was saying, *Just write, Tanya. Do it. Enjoy it. Don't make a big deal out of it. This is one of the things you were born to do. Just let go and speak your truth.* But from time to time my ego (or Gremlin) would catch wind of this conversation and jump in with all sorts of nasty commentary: *Who do you think you are? What makes you think you could do this? Do you think just anyone can do this? Look at these words; they're not good enough. You're not good enough and you never will be.*

Ouch. But I've come to recognize that little Gremlin ego and live with him. And practice fully seeing him, acknowledging his presence. *I see you. I'm acknowledging you little Gremlin ego. I know what you're doing and it's not going to work this time. I'm operating at a different frequency now and I'm in a better place. I don't need your commentary here anymore – you can go now.* And you know what? When we shine a light on that little fucker, it's like he sulks and slowly disappears into the walls. It doesn't mean he's gone forever.

No, he will always live within us. But it's about managing him and recognizing him for what he is and what he truly does.

He actually is there to help us in times when we're—oh, I don't know—walking down a dark alley and danger is close and we need to get away because he's the offspring of fear. And there is a time and a place for fear, but I'm not walking down any dark alleys any time soon so, *Thank you ego but you are free to leave now.* I got assertive with my ego. Who knew!? I spoke my truth to it. I kept on going with my heart's desires in spite of its negative commentary, and that is how I've learned to move through all those once paralyzing fears. Like what kept me pregnant with this book for nineteen years!

The practice of living purposefully—I was doing lots of that too. I had contributions that I was (and am) making them every day and sharing with those around me. I was putting energy behind my intentions and trying to put my best out there. As I write this book, I think of Georgia and Everett reading these words, and I hope they feel my love coming through these pages. This book is an act of love for them, for you, for everyone reading and absorbing these words. We're on this journey together, and it's my wish that as many people as possible feel empowered and inspired by even a few stories within this book—to bring you back to peace, to bring you back to balance, to bring you back to the glorious person you already are inside.

And the practice of personal integrity—well, with values like mine, saying what you'll do and doing what you say means a lot to me. I practice living in integrity every day. I value genuineness and the fact that I drive a ten-year-old car that's fully paid for speaks to this. I've known people who wrack up all kinds of debt buying stuff they don't need to make their socio-economic position look grander than it really is and the reason that has bothered me in the past is because it's out of alignment with reality. It's not a reflection of integrity.

And they are enough, new car or not. We are all enough—just standing still with our socks on. Hell, even barefoot.

So, learning about these pillars and then running through the current progress I had made on each one of them led me to another realization: I wasn't acknowledging my progress. Isn't it funny (read: sad) how we often draw so much attention to the negative—what we aren't doing right, what we haven't mastered yet, what we're struggling with—instead of acknowledging and ultimately energetically fueling what we're doing right? Oh, I hope through practice I get better at that! All this progress was right there, waiting for me to acknowledge, waiting for me to see it. Like Esther Hicks says, "Nothing you want is upstream." Everything we want is downstream. It's already there waiting for us to *see* it! Acknowledge it. Pick it up and own it. And it starts with accepting and loving ourselves. As I mentioned earlier, I'm very much still learning this too. But I figure I need to be a really good friend to myself—my best friend—because I'm going to live with myself for a very long time. My relationship with my highest self, which also encompasses the Divine (with a side of ego, but nothing I can't manage) could be the most important relationship I'll ever have.

CHAPTER 9 Reflections:

1. How do you practice loving and accepting yourself?
2. Vaginas are truly miraculous and awe-inspiring. Discuss.
3. If your vagina was a super hero ('cause she IS!), what would be her name?
4. What are some of the imperfections that make you perfectly, uniquely, beautifully you?
5. If you could go back to your five-year-old self, what would you say to that precious little one:
   - Your twelve-year-old self...
   - Your sixteen-year-old self...
   - Your twenty-one-year-old self...
   - Your thirty-year-old self...
   - As high as you'd like to go...
6. How have you honoured each of Nathanial Branden's six pillars of self-esteem? No act is too small.

10
Be Grateful and Filled with Awe and Wonder

"Gratitude unlocks the fullness of life. It turns what we have into enough, and more. It turns denial into acceptance, chaos to order, confusion to clarity. It can turn a meal into a feast, a house into a home, a stranger into a friend."

~MELODY BEATTIE

"Be grateful." How many of us grew up hearing this, often in the toy aisle when we realized our parents weren't going to buy us that shiny new gadget. We were told to be *grateful* for the dull one we had at home! It felt like such a guilt-ridden statement! When I was growing up, the phrase "be grateful" was used often and didn't leave the most positive memories in its wake. I'm not proud to admit that despite knowing better, in moments of weakness, I've carried on the tradition with my own children. I've been known to quip one such "be grateful" command in similar times of trial. I work hard. It irritates me when they don't appreciate things I've done for them. It's even more irritating when I realize it's *me* who isn't appreciating things. Bloody hell. Projections are the worst!

I writhe with the discipline of gratitude myself. I hear about how some people easily integrate the practice of gratitude into their daily lives and I'm so envious! There are stories out there of people gently waking to the sound of wind chimes, stretching, meditating, listening to beautifully moving hymns and writing in a gratitude journal while birds chirp, bees pollinate flowers and blades of grass grow. Or is it just a Facebook myth? I, on the other hand, wake up in a cold sweat to the kids scream-singing Christmas carols in July as they open and slam cupboard doors while making musical instruments out of beat-up recycling and our bone china. I'm only kidding. We don't have bone china. But the described chaos is pretty accurate. In our house, it's sport for one of our cherubs to put on a show at breakfast with the goal of making the other one laugh until they snort water out of their nose. I am grateful for that. Not the snorting, the laughter. But all that to say that life gets noisy and like a whirlwind sometimes, and it's hard to *think* let alone take a moment to take a deep breath, pause and be grateful for the new and ordinary-turned-extraordinary things right in front of our noses. I find it challenging just to stop sometimes. I often feel catapulted into my own reality the moment my kids walk through the door. I love my kids and spend many days missing them when they're at school. But when the first words they utter when they barrel through the door is, "Why did Georgia get a turn and not me?" my gratitude can take a backseat as I take on the role of referee. And whistle-blowing while trying to make a nutritious dinner (that at least one will likely turn their noses up to) is tough, especially when all I want to do is wash the day off my face and put on my pyjamas. And then it's often a race to feed them (swiftly, but not too quick as to promote an upset stomach or choking) so we can get back into the car and drive across town to the soccer field.

Sometimes I find it hard to be clear headed enough to thank the Universe for soccer lessons in the first place. But I know it's important. I know it's worthwhile. And I know it breeds more happiness and joy if I can find a moment—even in the bathroom—to take a deep breath, get in touch with my divinity and thank my Heavenly Mother and Father for the many blessings around me. I know my problems are of the first-world variety! And so as you can see, I'm very much in the process of working on this topic myself.

And then there's social media, which, for me anyway, can leave me feeling anything but grateful. In fact, it can quickly become a barrier to gratitude for me. I'm not immune to wanting to slam down my laptop lid at the sight of those "perfect" images and commentary of the Instagramed life, especially when I know they distort reality. In many ways, I feel like the way some people use social media to portray these falsities creates further distance and divide from their social networks instead of its intended use. To connect. To be real. I have deep respect for those who have the courage to put themselves out there with words and photos of the sticky-fingered, blurred, unfiltered, seemingly ordinary realities that we all know so well. That is poetry to me. And I believe it actually forms greater connection when someone shares and bears witness to that unfiltered truth. Warts transform into beauty marks in those moments.

But over the years, in my finer moments, I've come to understand the term "be grateful" in a new light. Something resonated for me when I heard the phrase "the attitude of gratitude" because it transformed a perceived command into a practice. Gratitude became a verb. And something I *chose* to do for its many benefits.

Look at any spiritual tradition and chances are it has a practice of gratitude. We are taught to "count our blessings" and open ourselves to taking in the blessings that surround us to help lift us out of restless feeling of not enough into the joy of sufficiency and a closeness to Source. It has the power to shift energy, even for those who aren't convinced of the spiritual or ethical benefits of this practice. Science demonstrates that the heartfelt expression of gratitude works. I was fascinated to learn that today's cutting-edge technology is able to scientifically measure gratitude and its benefits. Learning about this stuff helps remind me of the benefits of gratitude, especially when I'm having moments when my left-brain is begging for evidence to complement my faith.

HeartMath Institute®, a recognized leader in researching the physiology of human emotions for the past twenty years had gathered new findings regarding gratitude and appreciation. HeartMath Institute says that true feelings of gratitude, appreciation and other positive emotions can synchronize brain and heart rhythms, creating a body-wide shift to a scientifically measurable state called "coherence." Its sensitive instruments measure heart-rate variability to determine the coherence you experience during feelings of appreciation. It even shows up on an electrocardiogram (ECG)!

In this optimal state, the body's systems function more efficiently, generating a greater balance of emotions and increasing mental clarity and brain function.[53] HeartMath Institute can measure coherence to show heart, brain and nervous system interactions that are sensitive to changes in emotions. While someone is experiencing coherence, the heart rhythm appears as a smooth wave-like pattern on a heart rate variability (HRV) graph. Contrast coherence with incoherence, which is created by negative emotions such as frustration and anger. Incoherence can often disrupt the synchronization of the body's systems and create jagged or chaotic patterns on a graph.[54] It affects the whole body's ability to function optimally. And to me, that makes sense: just pay attention to how you're feeling physically when you're in a state of gratitude. When all the stars feel like they're aligned, you're relishing the moment, soaking up the sun and grateful for everything that *is* in that moment. I don't know about you, but for me, I must remind myself how I'm feeling physically in that moment because it's like there's no pain and no suffering. Everything feels at ease. I feel light and in flow with natural and divine order. I think that's how we're supposed to feel most of the time, and we can access those feelings when we develop a sense of gratitude.

You don't have to be happy to practice gratitude

Gratitude is like a muscle. The emotion you're feeling at the time doesn't affect how much stronger it gets when you're exercising it. If you don't feel like going to the gym and you go and work out anyway, your muscles are still going to feel the effect of going to the gym. When it comes to gratitude, even people who are grieving can still be grateful. In fact, it's shown to have a great impact on the healing process. "You can practice anytime—when you feel sorrow, great anxiety over a parent's imminent death, if you have a disabled child," Miriam Greenspan, psychologist and author of *Healing Through the Dark Emotions: The Wisdom of Grief, Fear, and Despair*, says. "Whatever one can muster at these points as a prayer of gratitude—okay, I'm still breathing, or I have friends who care about me—tips the experience from being immersed unmindfully in one's suffering to moving into the present moment with a more holistic perspective."

It may seem difficult to comprehend holding emotions that seem at odds with each other at the same time, but Greenspan describes a sort of magical combination that emerges from this polarity. "We see that there is suffering, but there is also this gratitude, and we can hold them together," she says. And as Brother David Stendl-Rast a Catholic Benedictine monk once said, "We're not grateful because we're happy. We're happy because we're grateful."

I was amazed to learn that HeartMath Institute's more advanced research suggests that gratitude is not simply a nice sentiment or feeling but that sustained feelings of gratitude have real benefits, including:

- Biochemical changes - Favourable changes in the body's biochemistry include improved hormonal balance and an increase in production of DHEA, the "anti-aging hormone." Practicing the attitude of gratitude could make you younger – who knew!?
- Increased positivity – University of California, Davis and the University of Miami researchers studied 157 individuals over thirteen days to discover that daily gratitude exercises can bring about a greater level of positive feelings.
- A boost to the immune system – Practicing gratitude causes an increase in the body of mucosal immuno-globulin (IgA) antibody, which serves as the first line of defense against pathogens, bacterium, virus, or other microorganism that can cause disease. Amazing!
- Emotional "compound interest"– The accumulated effect of sustained appreciation and gratitude is that these feelings, and coherence, are easier to recreate with continued practice. This is because experiencing an emotion reinforces the neural pathways of that particular emotion as it excites the brain, heart and nervous system. The downside is that you also can reinforce negative emotions.

Thankfully, our sincere self-evoked feelings of gratitude and appreciation can have these emotions take up their own positive psychophysiological residence in our bodies. Emotions are reflected in heart rhythms. Changing those rhythms can result in quick and substantial changes in whatever emotional state we may be experiencing at that time.

Gratitude Toolbox

While it can be challenging at times, I find it helpful to start creating some rituals or behaviours that serve as our own sort of gratitude toolbox to help us navigate how to inject more gratitude into our daily practices and routines. The HeartMath Institute recommends the following three-step appreciation exercise:

1. Take a few short appreciation breaks during the day.
2. During each break take one or two minutes to breathe deeply through the area of the heart.
3. While doing so, try to hold a sincere feeling of appreciation in your heart area. This can be appreciation for a family member, friend who helped you with something, a wonderful vacation or even the image of your youngster laughing so hard when drinking water that it snorts right out of their nose!

Can you imagine the transformation we could have on the world around us if we all did this? I can certainly think of a few board meetings that would have benefited from someone taking a time out to do an appreciation exercise. You just need a little time—two minutes even—Oprah talks about doing this kind of thing when she has been in an elevator on her way down to tape a show. The investment of two minutes to think about gratitude for three things—and the causes of those three things—can mean the difference between a rich life and a poor one. Gratitude primes the pump for a brighter day. It also aids our sense of being in a state of awe and wonder, which often leads to those blissed-out feelings.

Now the simplicity of this exercise could lead some people to thinking that it's not even worth doing. But Karen Elaine Jackson, author of *Awakening to Gratitude*, asks us to consider this: people are constantly worrying about things they don't have or things that haven't happened, consequently they rarely take stock of the beneficial things they do have and good things that have already happened. She says that if it's possible for even the simplest negative thought to provoke a change in mood then why not a positive grateful thought as well?

If you find it difficult to get going, Karen offers some suggestions. Of course, this is always a deeper, richer exercise if you can think of a few of your own:

- I don't have a headache today.
- I had a good breakfast.
- I have my family.
- My new socks keep my feet warm.
- I made a joke and people laughed (got to take whatever you can get!).

Some of these things may seem trivial but no grain of thankfulness is too small. And whenever I still have trouble getting there, I think of something kind I can do for someone. And then do it. Then after I've done that small gesture, I'm often thankful for my ability to be able to do that. That's a shortcut to gratitude. Now if the exercise starts to lose its power, it could be because of habituation. I try to be creative with my gratitude. It can be fun too! Here are a few other things that are helping me on this road to gratitude.

Keeping a gratitude journal

Other strategies to prolong the sense of gratitude include keeping a gratitude journal and writing in it daily or even weekly. Research has shown it works! In an experimental comparison conducted by Emmons & McCullough (2003),[55] those who kept gratitude journals on a weekly basis exercised more regularly, reported fewer physical symptoms, felt better about their lives as a whole and were more optimistic about the upcoming week compared with those who recorded hassles or neutral life events. Whoa!

Recalling joyful memories

A few summers ago, my family took a holiday to Prince Edward Island. We had started to read the book *Anne of Green Gables* before we left for our trip and finished it while we were there enjoying the red-sand beaches and all the delights that the island has to offer. Our son was six and our daughter four. They were fascinated with Anne. We even took them to Charlottetown to see the play. After the performance, the actress who played Anne was outside posing for photographs. My daughter was determined to meet her. I explained to her that we could do that, but I couldn't take her photo because I had forgotten my camera, to which she replied, "It's okay. I just want to give her a hug." And she did, practically leaping—in her frilly little blue dress—into Anne's arms. That actress was so receptive to her love, staying in character and truly giving back to a little girl who had only dreamt of such a moment. And that photograph will forever stay in my heart.

That night, after the kids went to bed, my husband and I were talking the day over on the veranda. Yes—there was a covered veranda! It was so picturesque. We had just finished reading *Anne of Green Gables* aloud to the kids that day and were a little sad to see the cover close. We asked ourselves what it was about Anne that made her so loveable and such a cherished character. We resolved that it was her gratitude for merely being alive. She came from a childhood of trauma but illuminated her way out of dark times by richly developing her imagination and finding the extraordinary in the seemingly ordinary. She ignited her senses and found beauty in nature, colours, smells and kindred spirit friendship. And as a result, she gave back to so many. Even the character of Marilla, grumpy and sour pre-Anne, couldn't help but love and cherish her "Anne-girl," and eventually her heart melted. When you're grateful, you can't help but give back just by being and appreciating what's right in front of you. Lucy Maud Montgomery wrote that book in 1908 and more than a century later, Anne Shirley continues to give back to others in spades.

Visual reminders

Visual reminders of gratitude have been shown through research to have an extraordinary effect on mood. For many, it might include pasting signs up by their desks or on the fridge to remind themselves of the importance of gratitude, because even thinking about someone you're grateful for can dramatically shift your mood. In fact, Emmons & McCullough's 2003 research also revealed that feelings of gratitude "may be beneficial to subjective emotional well-being."[56] For example, Watkins and colleagues (Watkins et al., 2003) had participants test a number of different gratitude exercises. One involved thinking or writing about a living person they were grateful for—some even wrote a letter to deliver to someone for whom they were grateful. After, participants were also asked to describe their living room. The results were remarkable.

Those who engaged in a gratitude exercise showed increases in their experiences of positive emotion immediately after the exercise, and this effect was strongest for participants who were asked to think about a person for whom they were grateful. Participants who had grateful personalities to begin with showed the greatest benefit from these gratitude exercises. In people who are grateful in general, life events have little influence on experienced gratitude (McCullough, Tsang & Emmons, 2004)[57].

We can all develop a practice of gratitude around these visual reminders. For example, we could post notes and quotes about gratitude on our bathroom mirrors and make a ritual of reading and saying them (in our heads!) while we're brushing our teeth or flossing. There are some beautiful thanksgiving and gratitude poems out there to revel in. What a wonderful way to start and end a day.

Saying grace

Gratitude is really the wellspring from which everything good flows. In my family, we say grace before meals and prayers at night with our kids. It gives them chances to practice gratitude and prompts us to practice it too. The key is to not let it get stale so as to turns into lip service or a dogma. I love when, in the summer months, my six-year-old gives thanks for our neighbours shovelling our driveway. (Yes, they do that – can you imagine?! We are truly blessed with wonderful neighbours.) Y'know, last winter. Or when my eight-year-old calls out specific Lego pieces that he's grateful for. It's a wonderful practice to bring to your family, to connect you and bring you back to that source. That wellspring. Because as parents, we often need those reminders just as much as our kids do. Life gets busy, so it's important to pause once in a while and give thanks and marvel at the wonder of the universe and those inhabitants within in it. It brings us to a place of awe, and I believe that's the space where the Divine wants us to dwell—in a place of gratitude, awe and wonder. Why else would this universe be filled with so much of it?

A state of awe and wonder

The other day we were driving with our kids in the car and a song came on the radio that had them belting out the words with such sweet and powerful conviction. Kids find joy naturally and we can learn so much from them. It's about being right here, right now in this moment and choosing to feed the light instead of the dark. There may be clouds in the sky—it's true—but look at what they offer, a contrast for us to be able to truly see so we can appreciate the blueness of the sky. Do you choose to focus on that one cloud—even a dark cloud—or the blue that surrounds it? It took me a long time to say and know this, but I choose blue. I choose to believe that whatever I feed will grow. It's like my vegetable garden. It's like my body. It's like my children. It's that old saying, "You reap what you sow." What you put in is what will come out and not always in the same exact place you planted it because the Universe has a way of nurturing those seeds and turning them into the most beautiful and magnificent fields.

It's our job to stay present, to notice, to let ourselves be in a state of gratitude, awe and wonder and to make a choice by asking ourselves, Do I want to stay here or do I want to go to that other place, a place of negativity, fear, perceived security, those places that I think will keep me safe at the cost of not fulfilling my soul? I remember writing articles and papers and speeches for other people instead of letting my own voice deliver me. That's the switch I continuously need to flip when I start going down that fear-doubt aisle: If

I keep feeding it, I will stay there. I need to let myself be free by trusting myself, letting myself be in the present, seeing the beauty and awe of nature and in those seemingly ordinary things around me: a blade of grass, the morning sun, the deep belly laugh of a child, the flowers that I admire that transform into vegetables in my garden. Those are the things I choose to focus on, and the more I do that, the more they grow. It is faith meshed with scientific fact. Yin and yang. Light and dark. It is truth and where I choose to live now. Do you?

It's important to seek out awe-inspiring moments in our everyday lives. That doesn't mean we need to climb summits or swim with dolphins each day to experience it. Even watching inspiring videos can do the trick of putting us into a state of awe and wonder. And think of how you feel after you watch videos like that or experience a sense of awe and wonder. You want to do good! You want to put more good out there. Imagine the impact on our world if each and every one of this did this each and every day.

Limitations are unnecessary killjoys. We need to challenge ourselves to reinvent our ceilings, or better yet, remove them altogether. We need to be grateful, to be present, to be in awe of the here and now with a deep knowing, or understanding, that the more attention we give those things, the more they will blossom and take up residence in our lives and in the world around us.

CHAPTER 10 Reflections:

1. How do you practice gratitude?
2. Are you giving gratitude enough space in your life? If not, how could you change that?
3. Describe a time when you have been in awe. What was that like? Is this a place you could go to in your mind the next time you're down or off centre?
4. How do you feel when you're in a space of gratitude?
5. What are three things you're grateful for right now?

11
Celebrate and Feel Good

"The more you praise and celebrate your life, the more there is in life to celebrate."

~ OPRAH WINFREY

There's no sense in working so hard and stretching to achieve small and great things when you don't stop to smell the roses and celebrate the milestones. And the word milestone is entirely up to you to define. My husband's Aunt Ivadelle was one of those larger-than-life personalities who had an opinion about everything bookended by a joke that you couldn't help but laugh at. In looks and demeanour, she reminded me of Olympia Dukakis, who played Clairee Belcher in *Steel Magnolias*.[58] Delicate as a flower, tough as steel and the life of the party, just like Aunt Ivadelle.

And oh, Ivadelle loved a good party. Just a bubble off plumb, she found a reason to celebrate whenever the urge seized her. Case in point, in 1991, she and my husband (her nephew) randomly decided to host a huge "17 and 51" party outdoors in a farmer's field, because honestly, why *wouldn't* you celebrate turning seventeen and fifty-one together in one jubilant union?

Robert's family has so many great memories from that party. Over the years, it's reminded us to celebrate the milestones, even the ones that don't end in zero or five or that you can necessarily find a Hallmark card for because it's an essential part of honouring your diva within. Ivadelle died in her seventy-first year. Imagine if she'd waited for some sort of socially acceptable seventy-fifth birthday milestone to celebrate her zest for life?

When I think of Aunt Ivadelle, I'm reminded to kick up my heels, fill up my cup and dance. She was funny as hell too. Once, at a girls' dinner she hosted at a cottage, she lifted up her napkin ring, turned to me with a straight face and said, "Is a table really a place to put a cock ring?" She taught me to celebrate the big and the small things and find occasion to celebrate. Some people are timid about throwing their own party. But honestly, do you think your guests are going to mind if you decide to give them food and drink and have a good laugh? And if they do, you've invited the wrong people. Celebrate it all. Laugh and have fun. Stop worrying about trying to make things perfect or appropriately timed. It doesn't need to be Martha Stewart approved. You know, toward the end of her life, Aunt Ivadelle shared that the most fun she said had ever had in her life was on the night I hosted a "Pirate Pub Crawl" in the small city of Stratford where we lived at the time. I organized the whole thing in about thirty minutes. I printed out a map of downtown, drew stars around different pubs on our trail and wrote out dares to complete at each one. For example, buying a stranger a shot of rum to swig together. Or walk down the sidewalk and look a stranger in the eye (the one eye, because the other was covered by an eye patch) and roar, "Arrghh!" Or request the song *"Sweet Caroline"* at a pub with live music and start a dance party with as many people as possible—okay, that one wasn't entirely pirate-themed, but it was fun! There was a group of us from my family and Robert's family who wore eye patches and pirate hats as we paraded around town and we had so much fun! For no apparent reason at all except for the joy of it! For the silliness of it. For the fun of it. And who knew it would result in the most fun one woman—life-of-the-party person, no less—would experience in all her seventy-one years?

With my friends, I often try to make up reasons to celebrate too. I like to create my own quirky milestones. For example, one night when I needed a really good laugh, I watched *Sisters*[59] starring Tina Fey and Amy Poehler. Total shine theory. I love those girls! That movie inspired an event to celebrate with my friends. It wasn't a milestone, but instead we celebrated the present moment. At the time, some of us were new mothers who needed a night out where there wasn't a child attached to our boob, whereas others wanted a break from chauffeuring kids to rep soccer while others were going through some heavy shit with aging parents, relationship woes and relatives with ailments. What did we all have in common? We all needed to shake our groove thangs and be free. Cut loose and cut some serious tile! So we turned it into an event called "We're Officially Cougars," and we wrapped that shit up in a bow and celebrated! Owned it! We dressed in leopard skin prints and teased our hair to look like *Peg Bundy*, and we went out to a bar in our city, one where we'd seen "cougars" in action when we were in our twenties, and we danced and were wild and free. I laughed myself dizzy! It was a great night. I love making up celebrations or celebrating random years. It's so much more freeing and gratifying and fun than celebrating "milestone" birthdays or anniversaries.

It's about celebrating life where we are right now. Even writing this book, when I'd finished Chapter 10, which I'd found difficult to write and knew that I only had a couple more chapters to go, I had to stop and look back at how far I had come. Nineteen years in the making, all the experiences

I had wracked up, the love, sweat and tears I had put into the pages of a book and putting myself out there; that was more than enough to celebrate!

Body, mind and spirit

When we were in India, my husband and I visited a university renowned for medicine. Our tour guide explained that when it was built, the school required that each physical space devoted to a classroom would be matched with an equal amount of space for an exercise field and another equal amount of sacred space for worship. The power of threes. The university itself had been around for more than a century. It was an early example of a living space that truly honoured the concept of body, mind and spirit. In India, these aren't "nice-to-haves;" they take this stuff very seriously. There's no use in saying you observe a balance of body, mind and spirit if you're not practicing it. And so they did. They would study for a certain period of time and then they would exercise in the field for that same amount of time and they would worship for that long as well. Again, Hinduism wasn't a dogma, it was a way of life. Hindus bring these principles into their daily practices and ways of being in this world.

I took a lot from that lesson and appreciate how it's not just an airy-fairy idea but a when-the-rubber-meets-the-road kind of practice. I like that it's even called a practice because that's a verb and can always be exercised and improved.

This morning while I was meditating, my son came into the room three times to get paper to draw on. The first time, I kept my eyes closed and gently told him that I was meditating and to quickly come in and get what he needed. I was still om-inspired at that point. By the third time, I opened my eyes, swung my head around and barked out that I was meditating and please give me a few minutes. Okay, not a proud Mama moment. The rest of the meditation went on fine but I could have gone deeper. But it's okay; it's practice (the mothering and the meditation!). I'm getting better all the time. I'm practising practice too. And working through distractions is helpful in my overall path of resilience.

I think that being mindful and living out a three-sliced pie chart where we're devoting time, resources and energy to body, mind and spirit is important. It's like a three-legged stool. Balance creates strength, and it allows us to live in flow. I think of this when I'm feeling out of balance and as a result, not feeling very good. I can often trace back my feelings to one of those three slices. There have been times when I was in Seminary or deep into religious or spiritual inquisition and learning where I felt like I was really honouring that part of me but still didn't feel that great. I've found that sometimes even the greatest spiritual places require other aspects to create a balanced state. This is why rituals such as yoga—exercising the body—are followed by meditation where we're exercising the spirit and calming the mind. It's all a state of flow. Similarly, there have been times when I've felt like I was honouring my body and feeding it nutritionally-dense foods and exercising it regularly, but I still felt like something was missing, possibly mental stimulation or a spiritual need that needed to be nourished.

For me, this whole body, mind, spirit connection falls in that order too. If I'm not feeling good physically, forget it. And on all three levels, it's like we're always reaching for new heights. Have you ever found that? You start eating healthily and then you have one day where you stuff your face with excess and you wake up the next morning and feel hungover even though you might not have had an ounce of alcohol? What the hell is that? I'll tell you what. It's your body's way of saying, "Na-ah! I deserve better than this and won't be treated this way anymore without retaliation, thank you very much."

And before you get mad at yourself or start quipping things like, "Who do you think you are, body?" REMEMBER: You built that body into the highly intelligent, highly functioning masterpiece that it is—okay maybe not alone (thanks be to God) but you upgraded it. And now the Cheetos and Truckdrivers you got by on in university just won't do anymore! It's like giving an extremely bright fifth-grader one of those cardboard baby books and expecting her to be thrilled, dazzled and intellectually fulfilled. Na-ah. And she'll be telling you about it too. That is good! That is body feedback, and it's a reminder that we are operating on a different level now. Even our energy force fields have evolved, and we need more of the real deal for where we're at. And that means nutritionally dense food for the body, mind and spirit.

The Other V-word: Shocking the body with whole, plant-based foods

A few weeks ago, I accidentally became a vegan.

There I was – minding my own business – when my husband asked if I wanted to watch a Netflix movie called, *'What the Health.*[60]

Sure – why not. "What the health!" I said. It was a Friday night, the kids were in bed, I'd just poured myself a glass of crisp white wine and I was so happy about all of the above that I would've said yes to just about anything. I had no idea what the movie was about, or what sort of changes would ensue. Only in hindsight did I realize that I was on the eve of something big.

If you had've told me the movie would lay out an argument so compelling and logical that I'd forgo my beloved cheese, I would've questioned your sanity. I've seen other movies like this before – and do you know what happened? Nothing! I was over it by happy hour. Um, did I tell you that I almost opened a cheese shop once? Cheese and dairy products in general (full fat, thank you very much) were my thing.

It's not that I was ignorant to the fact that veganism existed, I just didn't get it. It seemed so strict, complicated, joy-depriving and sometimes even a bit uppity. I chose to plug my ears and roll my eyes at anything that would jeopardize my little slice of pleasure.

And really – was veganism even healthy? What about protein? What about calcium? And B12! How could any responsible parent not give their children milk? And could we revisit pleasure? Did I tell you I wrote to Starbucks after it discontinued my egg and gouda artisanal breakfast sandwich because it was depriving me of my Friday morning joy? First-world problem, right?

Wrong.

In many ways, what's happening today is a first-, second- and third-world problem. It's a planet problem too.

What the Health opened my eyes to the fact that by adopting a plant-based diet, I could become significantly healthier, help my family live longer, help our exhausted earth and waters, and be kinder to our fellow mammals and creatures that also inhabit this planet.

Now, I can't do the movie justice – you really have to invest 90 minutes and watch it on Netflix or online to learn more – or to check out the facts at www.whatthehealthfilm.com/facts. And don't disregard the research because much of it is American; Canada isn't far behind. What really stood out of me was the link between meat and dairy to cancer, diabetes and cardiovascular disease. I had no idea that animal agriculture is responsible for eighteen per cent of all greenhouse gas emissions, which is more than the combined exhaust from all transportation. That doesn't even count the water it takes to grow the grain, the water it takes to feed the animal, or the operation of the feed mill, the farms, the slaughterhouses or the meat producing factories. Not to mention how we're treating animals. I feel lonely in admitting I'm not a huge 'animal lover' but I know cruelty when I see it. In all my cheese-loving days I didn't realize that on dairy farms, mother cows are taken away from their calves two hours after giving birth. And they mourn the loss of their babies, often staring in the direction that they last saw them and bellowing for weeks. As a mother, how could I do this to another mother? I just can't anymore. And then there's the trauma experienced by they young calves after losing their mother. It's all so heartbreaking.

We're producing and raising so many of these animals, that we're adding to the pollution of our waterways because we need a place for their poo! If we were to divert half the food we use to feed the animals we eat to the world's hungry, there would be enough for everyone. We never used to eat this much meat.

I also hadn't made the connection that many of the animals I was eating got their protein from...plants. And I don't need as much protein as I thought. And cow's milk is made for, like...baby cows, that will grow into ginormous cows. And B12 is a bacteria that we used to get through water, but in today's super-sterile world, we need to take it in a supplement, and yeah, I'll make sure our family gets it in a supplement. No big whoop. And oh – some of the world's fittest, healthiest ultra-men and women athletes get their strength, endurance and overall super-health from plant-based diets.

By the end of the movie, I wasn't grossed out; I was gobsmacked. With saucer eyes, I slowly turned to my husband and said in slow-mo, "I think I just became a vegan." I'm so glad he felt the same. It would be difficult to make a significant change without having the support of those closest to you. And if my husband – grandson of dairy farmers who grew up with a side-of-cow in the deep freeze at all times – could do it, anyone can.

We made a commitment to try out a plant-based diet. Since then, I've been experimenting with new recipes from *Oh, She Glows*, *Forks Over Knives*, *21-day vegan kickstart*, *DIY Vegan*, *The Kind Diet* and *Peas and Thank You*, to name a few. The library is stacked with all of these great reads.

We hosted our first vegan dinner party and it was a hit! So much fun to try out new recipes and see how others can find the deliciousness of it too. And guess what? Nut cheeses taste amazing! So does cashew cream (better than sour cream), homemade almond milk – I even made fermented nut cream cheese today! There are so many great non-dairy options that don't sacrifice heavenly taste.

Each week we've been discovering more related Netflix movies that have helped validate our choice: shows like *Cowspiracy*,[61] *Vegecated*,[62] *Forks Over Knives*,[63] *Food Matters*[64] and *Fat, Sick and Nearly Dead*.[65]

We're infusing our diets with more vegetables, fruits, legumes and whole grains. I almost can't wait to get my next set of blood work to see how my readings have improved. Even our kids are enjoying it! I'm amazed at how many new recipes they're trying. Our little square-foot-garden is helping too. And we continue to let the kids have choices: we've been buying plant-based foods to have in our house but if we're out or they're at a birthday party and want pepperoni and cheese pizza, for example, it's their empowered guilt-free choice.

Best of all, I feel awesome! I had no idea what it was like to wake up and not feel bloated. I didn't even know I was bloated ...like, 24-7! Now, I just feel good. I highly recommend checking out some of these documentaries, vegan cookbooks and giving plant-based eating a whirl. You might be surprised at how much good can come from this sort of shift.

Feeling good

Feeling good is the culmination of all we've covered from Chapter 1 to now. It starts by realizing that there is real, true-life divinity coursing through our veins because we contain part of the Great I Am. It's in our DNA. Once we know and fully honour that, it sets us on a path to uncover our gifts, what matters to us, and— with the right support, the right practices, the right levels of love and acceptance for ourselves and others—helps us choose how to live out our values. Feeling good is the result of celebrating our values, honouring who we are and ultimately giving back to others as we have been blessed (which I'll discuss in the next chapter).

Feeling good is a road. Things won't always be perfect. (Is anything perfect, really, except maybe God?) You'll run into setbacks along the way, but now you're equipped with tools to help you stop, assess where you are, be present in the moment, be in awe and appreciate the wonder of the world around you. You'll even be able to marvel at how your life consistently dances with grace because you are a spiritual being serving a higher being by honouring your calling. Taking all those steps feels so darn good, but we also have the opportunity to help others feel good.

Acts of kindness

I challenge everyone—including myself—to make a ritual to perform at least one act of kindness each day. When we close our eyes at night, we can reflect on what we've done and smile knowing that we did our work. We honoured the divinity that exists within us, and we can sleep peacefully knowing someone's life was slightly sweeter that day because of something we said, did or dreamed for them. Imagine how many mountains we could move if we all did these small and simple acts?

As women, we are powerful creatures. We give, nurture and sustain life. We can share our gifts and talents with others too so they can see what it's like to be mothered in a world that needs more nurturing, selfless acts of kindness and care. The world needs us and the time is now.

It's important to relish the good we're putting into the world so that we can cultivate more of those good feelings. Feeling good is not a selfish act. It radiates to all those around us. It gives others inspiration and permission to feel good themselves. Imagine a world where everyone felt good, where everyone felt free. Imagine how competition and hatred would diminish and dissolve all together if people were happy, content and free being their best and most powerful selves. They would feel so filled up that their chalice would run over with kindness and love and goodness and spill onto others around them. That's what happens. That's how we cultivate positive change in this world and harvest the pure and simple rewards.

Feeling good is a state of mind and a choice that starts with us and starts now. There is no waiting until we're at a particular age or stage in our lives or we have the right job, home or waistline. All that's irrelevant. What matters is this moment we have now. Right now. It's your eyes on this page, my fingers on this keyboard, connecting over something that's more powerful than us, something that's grounded in love, comfort and blessings.

Remembering all this stuff helps feed the goodness. Focus on the goodness. What we feed, grows. When we feed the worry or not-good-enough thoughts or lack, they grow too. It's so important to feed the good. When we feel good in our bodies, we'll end up feeling good all around.

I recently came across a BuzzFeed post entitled "29 Celebrities Who Will Make You Feel Good About Your Body."[66] It's coupled with some beautiful non-airbrushed images of the stars, which I love. I'm not someone who is transfixed by the whole celebrity culture, but to me, these people were very funny and made me laugh at a time when I was taking myself way too seriously. Here's the rundown of what they said:

1. "If we're regulating cigarettes and cuss words because of the effects it has on our younger generation, then why aren't we regulating things like calling people 'fat?'" – Jennifer Lawrence.
2. "My limbs work so I'm not going to complain about the way my body is shaped." – Drew Barrymore
3. "I'm not perfect. I have cellulite. So what." – Kim Kardashian
4. "Being called gorgeous is not a bad thing! But at the same time, I don't want to thrive on other people's opinions of me." – Lupita Nyong'o
5. "I love my snaggle fangs. They give me character and character is sexy." – Kirsten Dunst
6. "I think it's ridiculous that you need to look a certain way to be conventionally pretty." – Kristen Stewart
7. "Among my acquaintances, there is no woman wearing XS. No, sorry, there is one: my daughter. The point is that Mia is 11 years old." – Kate Winslet
8. "Being size 0 is a career in itself, so we shouldn't try to be like them. It's not realistic and it's not healthy." – Rihanna
9. "I've never had a problem with the way I look. I'd rather go for lunch with my friends than go to the gym." – Adele
10. "Even I don't wake up looking like Cindy Crawford." – Cindy Crawford

11. "If someone has a problem with a size 12 girl with no make-up on and a big spot on her chin, that's their issue." – Charlotte Church
12. "The female body is something that's so beautiful. I wish women would be proud of their bodies and not diss other women for being proud of theirs." – Christina Aguilera
13. "I think about my body as a tool to do the stuff I need to do, but it's not the be all and end all of my existence." – Lena Dunham
14. "I'm imperfect. The imperfections are there. People are going to see them. But I take the view you only live once." – Kate Hudson
15. "The most alluring thing a woman can have is confidence." – Beyoncé
16. "Who cares if there are lumps on my thighs. I'm guilty of having human legs that are made up of fat, muscle and skin and sometimes, when you sit, they get bumpy." - Kristen Bell
17. "Take your time and take your talent and figure out what you have to contribute to this world. And get over what the hell your butt looks like in those jeans." – America Ferrera
18. "Think outside of the box. Pledge that you will look in the mirror and find the unique beauty in you." – Tyra Banks
19. "I'm not a pin-up, thankfully. I am beautiful to my husband. I am beautiful to my friends. I feel sexy and all those things with the people I love." – Olivia Colman
20. Females are the most beautiful, gorgeous creatures in the whole world. And I think we are gorgeous no matter what size we are." – Alicia Keys
21. "I was one of the only girls at my school that didn't get a nose job. I'm proud to be a voice for girls and say,

'You don't need to look like everyone else. Love who you are." – Lea Michele

22. "I definitely have body issues but everybody does. When you come to the realization that everybody does – even the people that I consider flawless – then you can start to live with the way you are." – Taylor Swift
23. "We're always too skinny or too fat or too short or too tall. We're shaming each other and we're shaming ourselves and that sucks." – Emma Stone
24. "Young women, don't worry so much about your weight. What makes you different, or weird – that's your strength." – Meryl Streep
25. "I don't think you should criticize someone's body no matter what. My weight doesn't define who I am." – Chloe Kardashian
26. "I'm okay with having bad dance moves. I'm okay with having horrible lower teeth. That's what makes me me, and for some reason, it's worked out all right." – Katy Perry
27. "Even though it will never be flat again, my stomach is still my favourite because it reminds me of my greatest achievement: my babies." – Isla Fisher
28. "I'm a human being, an imperfect human being who's not made to look like a doll, and that who I am as a person is more important than whether I have a nice figure." – Emma Watson
29. "You can't really invest in your looks as the only thing because they're a depreciating asset. It's like putting money in a stock that's going down." – Rashida Jones
30. And finally, back to where we started things with Jennifer Lawrence and another brilliant quote of hers, "If anyone even tries to whisper the word 'diet,' I'm like, 'you can go fuck yourself."

CHAPTER 11 Reflections:

1. What's an upcoming random celebration, a milestone (or not) that doesn't end in a zero or five that you will look into planning a celebration around?
2. What are three ways you could start shocking your body with goodness?
3. What act of kindness did you conduct today? What kind act will you commit to doing tomorrow?
4. If you're having trouble getting into the groove of feeing good, I highly recommend getting some of these songs on your playlist and having a spontaneous dance party with yourself. You might even invite others to join in. Belt these out and own the words. It's truly therapy for the soul.
    - Meghan Trainor's song *"Watch Me Do,"* or *"Me Too"* or *"I Love Me"* (Clearly, I love Meghan Trainor.)
    - Katy Perry's *"Firework"*
    - Alicia Keys' *"This Girl is On Fire"*
    - Martina McBride's *"This One's For the Girls"*
    - Idina Menzel's *"Let it Go"* from the hit Disney movie.
    - Aretha Franklin's *"Respect"*
    - Lady Gaga's *"Born This Way"*
    - Natash Beddingfield's *"Unwritten"*
    - Almost anything by James Brown but obviously, *"I Feel Good"*

12
Give Back

"If I help one person out with getting through the struggles that I've had then I've done my job on this planet and this life."

~ DEMI LOVATO

There is no greater feeling in this world than the feeling of giving back or helping another person. It's an amazing feeling to help someone see something remarkable in themselves or a situation. It can come in the form of a laugh, a hug, or a casserole. A couple days after our son was born, our neighbour Lori called to ask when would be a good time to bring us a hot meal. I was flabbergasted. I felt so depleted after an arduous labour and trying to figure out how to do this whole mothering thing, and here was a woman who had been through it herself and who knew what mattered. She brought it over on a tray, starting with a salad and then a chicken dinner complete with mashed potatoes and stuffing. I mean, seriously. The ultimate comfort food. And it was hot! The food was hot. That alone made me weep. I was slowly starting down a path of not knowing what hot food was anymore (a trend that continued for years with little ones), and here it was in all its glory straight from the oven and piping hot. I couldn't stop crying as I ate it. I cried for her kindness and thoughtfulness and how she didn't have to do that but honoured the call like it was her duty. I wept because people had told me I'd have people bringing me food left right and centre, but they were only words. Two people did, including this girl from across the street who barely knew me. But she knew what it meant to her when someone brought her hot food after giving birth. The Universe shows up in mysterious places. I cried at the love and care I could taste in that meal. And it was even followed by (hot) apple crisp. Bawling at that point! And now, whenever I learn of a friend, neighbour or even acquaintance who has had a baby, I try to make them food too. Nothing says love and shows kindness like food.

I remember my kids had this Mercer Mayer book called *Grandma, Grandpa and Me*, and the story ends with Grandma winning the blue ribbon at the country fair because of her blueberry pie's secret ingredient: love. We'd always talk and joke about that with our kids. "Don't forget to add the secret ingredient," we'd say. "*Love!*" our kids would squeal back. But it's really not a joke. You can taste the difference between a dish someone has thrown together, or one that was put together by machines, and one where the person thought of you, sent you good thoughts and put love into your food. I am sure there is evidence out there that proves it, but I don't need it. I know it's true.

Lori gave to me and I gave to others in return. The act of giving ignites a chain reaction that we've all witnessed before. It's what gave birth to the whole concept of a role model, describing people who have led by example and modelled the way for others to see and understand and give them inspiration and permission to do the same. And every little bit helps, adds up and actually comes back to us.

GIVE BACK

I remember volunteering for a couple of different agencies when I was in my twenties. It wasn't anything that would have won me a Volunteer of the Year award, but one night a week I'd volunteer at the maternity ward of a hospital or a hospice. My role would shift from one agency to the other on alternate weeks. Like the role of many volunteers, my duties were far from glamorous. At the hospice, I would tidy up and make brochure packets for families. At the maternity ward I would make—well, I don't know what you'd even call them, but I would take extra-long maxi pads, cut them in such a way as to broaden their shape, soak them in water, roll them up and freeze them to create, well, a vag pack of sorts for new mothers who had just given birth the "natural" (oh, please) way and needed to comfort and repair their poor ol' lady bits after the assault they had just endured by squeezing a watermelon out of something the side of a lemon. Yep, those things. You've heard of Stars on Ice? This was more like Vag on Ice. Although, one could argue those vaginas were stars. I had no idea what I was doing at the time except following a strict set of instructions and packing the freezer with those babies like nobody's business. (Every other week I'd be amazed that we'd gone through that many vag packs, and I needed to make a whole other batch.) Sure enough, they were popular in the maternity ward. And, fast-forward twelve years later, when I gave birth to my son, I lay in a hospital bed and a sweet nurse came to me and placed one in my hand. She started with, "Now dear, this is a—"

"Vag pack," I said to her with a smile. "Well dear, I've never heard it called that before but yes, it is an ice pack that you scooch between your legs to help things heal down there..." she went on and I had to take a moment—before I buried that thing into my paper panties—to thank the volunteer who made that vag pack and thank my younger self for doing something she didn't understand or that didn't serve her in any way but that would come back to her in the end. This time, literally.

I'm sure there are lots of stories of giving back that happen in hospital settings. I recall another time, this one very sad and before my son was born, when I needed to have a D&C because of a miscarriage. It was such an awful, gut-wrenching time, and as I waited for surgery, I needed to stay in a room—a hallway really—on my own, without my husband or parents who sat nervously in the waiting room. The wait was long. I was distraught, and the kindest, most angelic nurse took care of me. I was convinced she really was an angel. She comforted me with her words and her actions and her message of hope. I felt like I was dreaming. Before and after the surgery, there she was, like a mother from heaven, telling me that it was going to be okay, that I was okay and not to lose faith or hope. I could have kissed that woman. I asked for her name so I could write her a thank you letter afterward. We often have no idea the impact that we have had on a person's life. I am sure there have been people along your path who you have served. You might have forgotten what you did or said, but they remember. They were changed because of *you*. They were renewed, restored and given a message of love, light and hope. The best such stories come from those who have no vested interest in helping a person but they have gifts and talents to share and they just do. Because that's what they do. To think of the profound effect that has on our world takes my breath away.

They're often small but mighty acts. Sometimes it comes down to listening. The world needs more listeners to bear witness to someone's truth. Sometimes we don't need to say or do anything at all. We just need to be there in a nursing home, listening to a woman or man share the stories of their youth, listening as they describe their joys and heartaches and what scares them about the next chapter of their lives and what gives them peace. The same is true for children. We're often so quick to jump in and finish their sentences when they're struggling for the words, but those blessed little creatures are so close to Source and have so much wisdom to share with us. We need to let them speak. We need to listen as they feel, describe and illuminate the world with their truth.

My dear friend Suz came with me to hold my hand when doctors needed to check the levels of my hormones the time I thought I was having a miscarriage with what turned out to be Georgia (in all her glory!). My husband was on his way home from a business trip, so I didn't have his physical support. Suz and I barely spoke. I was too upset for conversation. She just held my hand and sat with me as I rested my head on her shoulder. What an act of pure selfless kindness. What an act of pure love. What an impact that had on me—how that taught me about divinity being alive and present in the world that surrounded me. It's like God called on Suz to do just that and she listened and rose to the call to give me a beautiful and much-needed gift.

It's about all the small and sometimes random acts that often don't take much effort but have a powerful and transformative impact on a person or situation. Giving gently used maternity clothes to a women's shelter for young mothers, donating kids' clothing and household items to charities instead of having a garage sale, giving to food drives, listening to a friend, feeding a stranger's parking meter. All those little things add up. And let's be honest, they give something back to us immediately too. Typically, we instantly feel good when we perform these good deeds, don't we? I always do! It's like a rush of quiet delight I allow to course through my veins. I don't need to tell anyone about it, but I need to feel it. Because feeling it feels good, it encourages me to do more of it.

It's part of our Divine Feminine nature to give back, to return to Gaia Sophia, the spirit name of our Mother Earth, the feminine side of God, and bring the gifts that we were naturally blessed with and share them with the world. Women need to stop acting like men living in a patriarchal world. Women need to act like the women they are, working with men to bring this world back to balance and harmony. We need to stop settling for something other than our heart's true desires because settling leads to mediocrity and quiet desperation. We need to grab hold of that sense of awareness through the quiet practice of meditation and being present, to understand the support we need to help us go for what truly makes our hearts sing. We need to be empowered and give back by encouraging others to do the same. This is our torch. This is the flame that we need to keep burning for the sake of our sisters and daughters and granddaughters. They are observing us. They are asking about us. They are curious about what we did, how we overcame obstacles, what our mantras were, what we had the courage to do or say or be in this world. They are curious about who we had the courage to love or support or inspire, how we were kind or grateful for our blessings. They are curious about how we moved through uncertainty, how we dug deep to uncover and bask in our faith, how we kept from going down the wrong paths by staying true to ourselves, our values and having the courage to speak our truth.

Unleash your sacred wisdom and power

I started this book by talking about all manner of boxes—Pandora's, exclusive theology, our own boxes—and unleashing the wisdom and power that has always been ours. The truth is that there was no box in the beginning. In the beginning, there was a woman named Pandora whose name means 'all-gifted.' She had a long list of virtues. She had unparalleled beauty, musical talent, a gift for healing, charm, boldness, dexterity, wit, curiosity, and even master gardener tendencies, for heaven's sake! But there was no box in the beginning.

Erasmus of Rotterdam created the box as a reflection of what was happening with women in society in Middle Ages. It's a phenomenon that had started much earlier than that. Even the Babylonians used to create idols out of metals or wood that would come out of or into a box when it was considered convenient to them. See, they even tried to put God in a box! But those people couldn't contain women or God in a box! And neither should we. We took on the role of creating the boxes after that. We boxed ourselves in. But even after those boxes were created, there was still hope. It's like the Divine Feminine stepped into that Erasmus myth and set the record straight: even if we create these boxes, there is always hope. And Divine Feminine wisdom. That is our birthright. It is what we were put on this earth to possess and use as a force for change and a force for good.

You are my sisters, and we each contain a piece of this wild, wise and divine power. When we stand together, it is stronger, louder and we can do more with it. We can use it for good. We can comfort, protect and inspire. We can share our wisdom with others and bear witness when we see it come through the people in our lives. We can unlock our potential together so that one day my daughter, my daughter's daughter and all the young women coming up the path won't even know what it's like to feel reserved, unheard, unimportant, and unworthy.

They will know, at an early age, that they are so precious and loveable and that there is divinity coursing through their veins. They will know that God is not male or female—God is both. They will know about the Divine Feminine qualities they possess and have possessed since birth and throughout the ages. The mantra, "You Go Girl!" will be like breathing. So will "Cheers to my Vagina!" They will feel free and strong and loved and shine, shine, shine all the glorious qualities and gifts they have been blessed with. And they will know that they have a responsibility to honour their whole selves, their truth and encourage others in their tribes to do the same.

And when they close their eyes at night and reflect on the events of the day, they will feel my love. They will feel your love. They will feel the sister love that is wired throughout the universe. Radiant beams of light. Hope. Infinite hope. And Divine Love at the heart of it all.

CHAPTER 12 Reflections:

1. Describe a time when someone gave you something that inspired you to give. Describe a time when you did something for someone that inspired them to give to someone else.
2. How could you—or have you—used your talents, gifts and presence to others?
3. If someone put a microphone in your hands right now and asked you to address a graduating class of young women, what would you say to them?
4. What excites you about unleashing your Divine Feminine wisdom and power? Is there anything that scares you about it?
5. What are three things you could do this week to live in this place of power?
6. Plan a get together with your most sass-tacular girlfriends so you can talk about all this good stuff, light your own fires, and last but not least...

CHEERS TO YOUR VAGINAS!

Be part of the sisterhood at tanyasood.com

Acknowledgements

I am eternally grateful for the nineteen-year journey that brought me to completing this work. Don't get me wrong, I stuck my tongue out and threw a hissy fit at it many times along the way, but it brought me to some truly remarkable people who have coloured my path and my life in the most beautiful way. The experience of knowing and spending time with them helped me tremendously.

I couldn't have written this book without the love, support and encouragement of my amazing husband, Robert. Throughout the seventeen years we've known each other, he hasn't stopped taking my breath away. I have been thoroughly sustained by his love, gentleness, kindness, respect for my work and commitment to our family. I'm equally grateful for the phenomenal father he is to our children and his ability to make me laugh so hard I can't breathe and I pee a little.

My children, Everett and Georgia, are real-life examples of 'awe and wonder.' They fill my life with love and laughter. They keep me grounded and teach me many powerful lessons each and every day. Like how beautiful a blade of grass or a grain of sand is. And how to not take life, or myself, too seriously. I am honoured and grateful beyond measure by the gift of being their mother.

My parents, Carrol and Gary, have shown me love, humour and resourcefulness throughout my life, among other things. They came from two different parts of the world and fought in the name of love to be together at a time that was unaccepting of differences – an important reminder for this day and age too. They came to Canada with $17, a hope and a prayer and one by one, step by step, they made a beautiful life for us. I love them both and I'm so grateful for their acceptance and support.

My brother, Justin, and sister-in-law, Lindy have been amazing. Their excitement and interest in my work make me smile. They are such positive forces in my life and even though we see some things differently, I love how we support each other so fiercely. I also love how we laugh "like nuts" (as Georgia would say) at the stupidest things. It's so awesome. They're so awesome. With such wonderful parents on both sides, it's easy to see where they got it.

To my extended family, including the Robinsons. Auntie Eda and Uncle Jim are like a second set of parents to me and I love them immensely. They make me feel loved, accepted and a part of the family. They're always there with supportive words and encouragement. The world is a better place with them in it. As for my Grandma, I don't even know where to begin. She makes eighty-five look like a piece of cake and I love how we've loved each other and shared so much laughter and fun throughout the years. I've never met a woman with so many boisterous songs, jigs and costumes. And don't even get me started on the soda bread. I will always look up to her and she will be forever tucked tenderly into my heart.

When I married Robert, I inherited a wonderful extended family. Thank you to the whole gaggle for many years of love and laughter. Becky and David been such positive supporters and I'm so grateful for how we raise each other up. David built our beautiful raised bed vegetable garden, and he introduced me to a cherished friend. Paul and Melissa have been a constant in my life since Robert and I started dating and we've shared so much laughter and fun together. Thank you to this big ol' family – living and those onto-the-next-party – for our many gatherings, all the food, all the support, and all the laughs we've shared throughout the years.

I'm deeply thankful for my life coach, Guy Reichard, and his vital role in helping me bring this book out into the world. Guy has taught me so much about life and what really matters. He has been a major sign-post in my life and he's walked me through some of the most profound exercises that helped me discover not only what I want and where I need to go, but who I really am. Thank you for helping me uncover the roadblocks – the biggest being fear – that were getting in the way of my most authentic path. His kindness, compassion and powerful wisdom will be with me always.

I extend my gratitude to my dear friend, Amy, who has been such a force of love and light in my life. Thank you for encouraging me, thank you for laughing with me about the most grade-eight stuff that sends me into laugh attacks, often right on her massage table. Thank you for caring for me, for helping me, for loving me and for radiating your goodness into the world by sheer matter of breathing. She is positively lovely and I love her.

I am overjoyed by the opportunity to work with an outstanding editor, Cristen Iris, and for all the gentle but powerful questions she raised along the way to make this book better. I can already tell that if we lived closer, we would hang out – a lot. Her kindness, sense of humour, grace and encouragement have uplifted not only this book, but me too.

Thank you to my Tellwell team, which was gracious, creative, supportive and amazing to work with.

Thank you to my girlz: Shelley, Jenna, Suz, Erica, Ang, Gayla, Lori, Judy, Kristin, Sarah, Heidie and even Greg, Mark and Lance, for being my soul sisters on this journey. You have made such a tremendous difference in my life and I love all the fun, silly pranks and belly laughter we share. Thank you to all those who have shown me the power of sisterhood. You are beautiful and I love you to pieces.

To the vivacious women leaders who I have had the pleasure of working with and learning from throughout my career: Veronique, Brigitte, Isabelle, Adele, Sandy and Alison. I'm ever inspired by their leadership.

To Pastor Doug and Sharon for their spiritual teachings, friendship and for all the encouragement, support, love and laughter they've shared. To Carol for sharing her spiritual gifts, intuition, love, light, laughter and care for me over the years.

To Bob, who allowed me to interview him and learn from his mind-bending wisdom.

To my writing (and life) teachers: Mrs. Sylvia Knight, Mrs. Barb 'Show-me-don't-tell-me' Carter and Sue McEwan who saw my gifts long before I did. To Mr. Brent Pavey for teaching me so many important life lessons and inspiring me to make a difference (like he had in my life). And my journalism instructors, Cathy Dunphy, Tim Falconer and Joyce Smith for pushing me (in a good way) to reach my potential, and for the amazing group of peers I shared the classroom with.

And to the girls coming up the path who inspire me to keep on keeping on.

I am ever grateful for each and every one of you.

Finally, thank you, Divine Mother, for your gentle but fierce love and for helping me find you, dwelling inside 'He' and dwelling inside me... all along.

About the Author

Photo credit: Holly Schnider
Used with permission

Tanya Sood is an award-winning writer, speaker and inspirer, whose purpose is to help women recognize the Divine Feminine wisdom and power that course through their veins – and own it.

Her Political Science degree from the University of Waterloo helped her become a more informed citizen of the world. Her Journalism degree from Ryerson University taught her to write and publish more than one hundred newspaper and magazine articles. Her Strategic Communications certificate from the University of Toronto increased her confidence so that she could move into senior leadership roles at a university, leading financial services institutions and child welfare services to powerfully influence others. And her time at Waterloo Lutheran Seminary gave her life more meaning, revealing three commanding truths: Divine love is the life force at the heart of humanity, far too many female leaders and references have been removed or excluded from sacred text, and that God is not male or female – God is God and God is both. She also grew up with an East Indian Sikh father and British Protestant mother, which has given her an interesting perspective on faith, spirituality and finding grace in middle ground.

Realizing that a Divine Mother exists as much as a Divine Father has rocked Tanya's world. She stopped searching for mothering qualities and influences, and she stopped feeling ashamed for wanting deeper mothering as a full-grown adult. She overcame three devastating miscarriages before being blessed with two miracles in the form of children and the privilege of mothering them. Her path led her to the wellspring of truth that the Divine Mother has been with her all along. By getting quiet and intentional, she started to hear Her voice.

Tanya wants to help others hear it too.

In her first book, *She Has Risen: Resurrect Your Divine Feminine Wisdom and Celebrate Your Miraculous Girly Bits*, Tanya helps women acknowledge their divinity, understand their values, assemble a sisterhood, love and accept their sultry selves, have faith, celebrate all manner of things and give back. She approaches each of these important, relevant and timely topics with humour and wisdom.

Tanya lives in Waterloo, Ontario with her kind, strong and devoted husband, Robert, and their two loving, inquisitive and ever-teaching children, Everett and Georgia.

Bibliography

Ackroyd, Eric. *Divinity in Things: Religion Without Myth*. Sussex Academic Press, 2009.

Axworthy, Nicole and Pitman, Lisa. *DIY Vegan: More Than 100 Easy Recipes to Create an Awesome Plant-based Pantry*. St. Martin's Griffin, 2015.

Beak, Sera. *Red, Hot and Holy: A Heretic's Love Story*. Sounds True, Inc., 2013.

Bradshaw, John. *Home Coming: Reclaiming and Championing Your Inner Child*. Bantam Books, 1992.

Brown, Dan. *The Da Vinci Code: A Novel*. Doubleday, 2013.

Diamant, Anita. *The Red Tent*. New York, NY: A Wyatt Book for St. Martin's Press, 1997.

Greenspan, Miriam. *Healing through the dark emotions: The wisdom of grief, fear and despair*. Shambhala Publications, 2004.

Hawkins, David. *Letting Go: The Pathway to Surrender*. Hay House Publishing, 2012.

Jackson, Karen Elaine. *Awakening to Gratitude*. The Gratitude Power Foundation, 2010.

Jacobovici, Simcha & Wilson, Barrie. *The Lost Gospel: Decoding the Ancient Text that Reveals Jesus' Marriage to Mary the Magdalene*. HarperCollins Publishers Ltd., 2014.

Jakes. T.D. *Instinct: The Power to Unleash Your Inborn Drive*. FaithWords Publishing and Hachette Audio, 2014.

Kagiso Msimango. *The Goddess Bootcamp: Okay is a Four-Letter Word – You Are Meant for More*. MFBooks Joburg – An Imprint of Jacana Media (Pty) Ltd., 2012.

Lessing, Doris. *The Black Madonna*. Panther Books Ltd., 1974.

Liddon, Angela. *The Oh She Glows Cookbook*. Penguin Random House Penguin Canada, 2014.

MacKenzie Brown, Cheever. *God as Mother: A Feminine Theology in India*. Claude Stark & Co., 1974

Maisch, Ingrid. *Mary Magdalene: The Image of a Woman through the Centuries*. The Liturgical Press, 1998.

Matheny, Sarah. *Peas and Thank You: Simple Meatless Meals the Whole Family Will Love*. Harlequin Enterprises Limited, 2001.

Mayer, Mercer. *Grandma, Grandpa and Me*. HarperFestival, 2007.

Moltmann-Wendel, Elisabeth. *The Women Around Jesus*. The Crossroad Publishing Company, 1982.

Montgomery, Lucy Maud. Devereux, Cecily Margaret, ed. *Anne of Green Gables*. Broadview Press, 2004 [1908].

Newberg, Andrew and Waldman, Mark Robert. *Words Can Change Your Brain*. Plume by the Penguin Group, 2013.

Picknett, Lynn. *Mary Magdalene: Christianity's Hidden Goddess*. New York, NY: Carroll & Graff Publishers, 2003.

Radford Ruether, Rosemary. *Goddesses and the Divine Feminine: A Western Religious History*. University of California Press, 2005.

Reichard, Guy. "*Values Clarification Exercise.*" www.coachingbreakthroughs.ca. PDF. 2016.

Ries, Eric. *The Lean Startup: How Today's Entrepreneurs Use Continuous Innovation to Create Radically Successful Businesses.* Crown Publishing Group, 2011.

Shelby Spong, John. *Born of a Woman: A Bishop Rethinks the Birth of Jesus.* HarperSanfFrancisco, 1992.

Silverstone, Alicia. *The Kind Diet.* Rodale Books, 2009.

Sroufe, Del. *Forks Over Knives – The Cookbook: Over 300 Recipes for Plant-based Eating All Through the Year.* The Experiment, 2012.

Stryker, Rod. *The Four Desires: Creating a Life of Purpose, Happiness, Prosperity and Freedom.* Delacourt Press, 2011.

Therese Winter, Miriam. *Woman Wisdom: A Feminist Lectionary and Psalter. Women of the Hebew Scriptures.* The Crossroad Publishing Company, 1991.

Ward Jouve, Nicole. *Female Genesis: Creativity, Self and Gender.* St. Martin's Press, Scholarly and Reference Division, 1998.

Watterson, Meggan. *Reveal: A Sacred Manual for Getting Spiritually Naked.* Hay House Inc., 2013.

Web Resources:

- news.harvard.edu/gazette/story/2010/11/wandering-mind-not-a-happy-mind/
- www.headspace.com
- fragrantheart.com
- www.mindful.org
- http://psychcentral.com/lib/growing-healthy-friendships/
- www.ted.com
- www.adishakti.org/_/divine_mother_ricky_hoyt.htm#sthash.QUJN1laP.dpuf
- www.theconnection.tv

- www.nytimes.com/packages/html/movies/bestpictures/rocky-ar.html
- http://wildgoddesslife.com/the-new-divine-feminine/
- https://mic.com/articles/119292/how-strong-female-friendships-help-women-get-ahead#.vOisd4VYN
- http://nymag.com/thecut/2013/05/shine-theory-how-to-stop-female-competition.html
- http://claireobeid.com/learn-how-to-receive/
- https://theconnection.tv/the-amazing-health-benefits-of-awe-and-wonder/
- whats-your-sign.com
- www.babycenter.ca/baby-names-finder

Notes

1. Coogan, Michael David, Marc Zvi Brettler, Carol A. Newsom, and Pheme Perkins. *The New Oxford Annotated Bible with the Apocryphal/Deuterocanonical Books: New Revised Standard Version.* Oxford University Press, 2007.
2. Ibid.
3. Ibid.
4. Ibid.
5. Ibid.
6. Ibid.
7. Bess, Savitri L. *The Path of the Mother.* Ballantine Wellspring: The Random House Publishing Group, 2000.
8. Kimsey-House, Henry, Karen Kimsey-House, and Phil Sandahl. *Co-active Coaching: Changing Business, Transforming Lives*, 2011.
9. Wolkin, Jennifer. "How the Brain Changes When you Meditate: By Charting New Pathways in the Brain, Mindfulness can Change Banter Inside Our Heads from Chaotic to Calm." *Mindful Magazine* September 20, 2015, web article.
10. Ibid.
11. Bradt, Steve. "Wandering Mind Not a Happy Mind: About 47% of Waking Hours Spent Thinking About What Isn't Going On." *Harvard Gazette* November 11, 2010, web article.

12. Ibid.
13. Newberg, Andrew and Waldman, Mark Robert. Words Can Change Your Brain. (2013), pg. 2.
14. Coogan, Michael David, Marc Zvi Brettler, Carol A. Newsom, and Pheme Perkins. *The New Oxford Annotated Bible with the Apocryphal/Deuterocanonical Books: New Revised Standard Version*. Oxford University Press, 2007.
15. Barber, Katherine. *The Canadian Oxford dictionary*. Oxford University Press, 1998.
16. Ibid.
17. Zarya, Valentina. "The Percentage of Female CEOs in the Fortune 500 Drops to 4%." *Fortune 500 Magazine* June 6, 2016, web article.
18. Toller, Carol. "Isabelle Hudon Says it's Lonely at the Top and it's Worth It: No, You Can't Have it All." *Canadian Business Magazine* October 6, 2013, web article.
19. Lao-tzu. & Mitchell, S. *Tao te ching: A new English version*. Harper & Row, 1988.
20. "The Power of Intention." *Success Magazine* July 2017, reprinted with permission on www.drwaynedyer.com/press/power-intention/
21. Ibid.
22. Ibid.
23. Stryker, Rod. The Four Desires: Creating a life of purpose, happiness, prosperity and freedom. (2011). New York, NY: Delacourt Press.
24. Didion, Joan. *The White Album*. Simon & Schuster, 1979.
25. Barber, Katherine. *The Canadian Oxford dictionary*. Oxford University Press, 1998.
26. Chris Buck and Jennifer Lee. Walt Disney Pictures. Walt Disney Animation Studios, 2013. Film.
27. Alan Parker. Bueno Vista Pictures, 1996. Film.
28. McIntire, Kathleen. "Meditation: Into the Lap of the Divine Mother." Online video clip. YouTube, September 9, 2009. Web. August 22, 2017.
29. Chris Buck and Jennifer Lee. Walt Disney Pictures. Walt Disney Animation Studios, 2013. Film.
30. Mike Gabriel and Eric Goldberg. Walt Disney Pictures, Walt Disney Feature Animation, 1995. Film.

31. Mark Andrews and Brenda Chapman. Walt Disney Pictures, Pixar Animation Studios, 2012. Film.
32. Ron Clements and John Musker. Walt Disney Pictures, Walt Disney Animation Studios, 2016. Film.
33. *A League of Their Own*. Penny Marshall. Columbia Pictures, 1992, Film.
34. *It's Complicated*. Nancy Meyers. Universal Pictures, 2009, Film.
35. OWN. "Bishop T.D. Jakes: Learning Instinct from Sea Turtles. Oprah's Life Class, Oprah Winfrey Network. YouTube, May 12, 2014. Web. August 22, 2017.
36. Carson, Rick. *Taming Your Gremlin: A Surprisingly Simple Method for Getting Out of Your Own Way*. William Morrow: An Imprint of HarperCollinsPublishers, 2003.
37. Shelby Spong, John. *Born of a Woman: A Bishop Rethinks the Birth of Jesus*. HarperSanFrancisco, 1992.
38. Ibid.
39. "Goddess: The Great Goddess." *Museum of Ancient and Modern Art: Recipient of the Excellence in Arts Education Award*, 2010. Web. August 22, 2017.
40. Hoydt, Ricky. "The Divine Mother." Adishakti.org, 2006. Web. August 23, 2017.
41. Ibid.
42. Ibid.
43. Ibid.
44. Ibid.
45. Ibid.
46. Ibid.
47. Ibid.
48. Dooley, Mike. "Notes from the Universe." Tut.com, August 4, 2016. Web. August 23, 2017.
49. Lies, Eric. *The Lean Startup: How Today's Entrepreneurs Use Continuous Innovation to Create Radically Successful Businesses*. Crown Business: an Imprint of the Crown Publishing Group, a Division of Random House Inc., 2011.
50. Coogan, Michael David, Marc Zvi Brettler, Carol A. Newsom, and Pheme Perkins. *The New Oxford Annotated Bible with the*

Apocryphal/Deuterocanonical Books: New Revised Standard Version. Oxford University Press, 2007.

51. Morley, Christopher. "To A Child." Chimney Smoke. George H. Doran Company, 1921.
52. Branden, Nathanial. *The Six Pillars of Self-Esteem: The definitive work on self-esteem by the leading pioneer in the field.* Bantam Books, 1995.
53. "The Science Behind the emWave® and Inner Balance™ Technologies. *HeartMath Institute,* 2017. Web. August 23, 2017.
54. Ibid.
55. Emmons, Robert, PhD. "Gratitude and Well-being." *Emmons Lab,* 2003. Web. August 23, 2017.
56. Ibid.
57. Ibid.
58. *Steel Magnolias.* Ross Herbert. TriStar Pictures, 1989, Film.
59. Sisters. Jason Moore. Universal Pictures, 2015, Film.
60. *What the Health.* Kip Andersen and Keegan Kuhn, A.U.M. Films & Media, 2017, Documentary Film.
61. *Cowspiracy: The Sustainability Secret.* Kip Andersen and Keegan Kuhn, A.U.M. Films: First Spark Media, 2014, Documentary Film.
62. *Vegecated.* Marisa Miller Wolfson. GetVegucated.com, 2011, Documentary Film.
63. *Forks Over Knives.* Lee Fulkerson. Virgil Films and Entertainment, 2011, Documentary Film.
64. *Food Matters.* James Colquhoun and Carlo Lesdesma. FMTV, 2008.
65. *Fat, Sick and Nearly Dead.* Joe Cross. Reboot Media, 2010.
66. Woodward, Ellie. "29 Celebrities Who Will Make You Feel Good About Your Body." *Buzzfeed.com,* May 22, 2014. Web. August 23, 2017.

CPSIA information can be obtained
at www.ICGtesting.com
Printed in the USA
LVOW11s2015191017
553053LV00001B/2/P